"What's a good route for me to take, so that I can see as much of Scotland as possible in a few days?" I've lost count of the number of times that I've been asked that question. My answer is always the same. I suggest that the visitor doesn't even try to travel around "seeing the sights". The finest way in which to see Scotland—or any other country, for that matter—is to wander around in a small radius, finding the small things as well as the large ones, for pins can often be as interesting as pyramids. Above all, a visitor who wants to get the most out of his time in another country must get to know the people. He can't hope to do this by driving past them.

I have tried to show something of Scotland's history which lies by the roadsides and, no less, in attics and barns. I hope that it may encourage people to linger on their travels through the country and to look for small things—and big ones, too—which tell stories clearly and delightfully to anyone who isn't in too much of a hurry.

My own interest in the by-ways of history is entirely due to having been taken in hand, when I was very young, by Mr A.O. Curle. He was an archaeologist of enormous erudition who was never too occupied to spare hours of his time in taking a small boy by the hand to show him what was lying unnoticed at his feet. He would pick up or point to something and would start asking questions. "What do you think this is?" "What was it used for?" "What sort of person would have used it?" He would go on with, "Yes, I know what it is, but I want you to work it out for yourself. Now . . . " and he would prompt, suggest and encourage the working out of the problem, always patient and inspiring a "satiable curtiosity" like that of the Elephant's Child. I hope that something in this *Scrapbook* may serve to spark off the same interest in someone else that, all those years ago, Mr Curle taught me.

I am most grateful to those people who have so kindly allowed me to photograph some of their own and their family possessions. I owe, too, a warm debt of gratitude to the Curators who have permitted me to make pictures of exhibits under their care. The Curator of Huntly House, in Edinburgh's Canongate; the Committee of the Weaver's Cottage in Kilbarchan; Mr Alec MacRae of the Clan Donnachaidh Museum near the Falls of Bruar, who is honorary piper to the Clan Robertson; and, too, to the late Captain James Macdonald, the former Curator of our own Clan Macpherson Association's Museum in Newtonmore.

Thanks must go, too, to Frang Mac Thomais, my good friend in Inverness, who not only set me the task of preparing this *Scrapbook* but has seen to it that I have kept on with the job. To my wife, Sheila, I owe more than just thanks. She has patiently ploughed through each and every one of the miscellany of articles, correcting mis-spellings and slips, sorting out references and preparing the index. Without her patient help, the **book** would never have been finished.

HARVEY MACPHERSON.

FOR SOMEBODY SPECIAL WHO LOVES PINK ELEPHANTS.

Contents

STONES

CAIRN OF THE SOLDIER'S WIFE *on Wade's Corrieyarrick Road. A.86 to Laggan Bridge, right-hand road at fork by shop and follow unclassified road 8 miles to farmhouse (unoccupied) where gate closes road. Thence 4 miles by foot.*
(O.S. Sheet 36: 448965)

THE CAIRNS OF REMEMBRANCE

It has been a Gaelic custom, since time immemorial, to raise a cairn of loose stones in order to commemorate happenings which people feel should not be forgotten. These cairns are, of course, completely informal and differ altogether from the large erections of cemented stone which, as permanent cairns, are built as memorials and which usually bear the embellishment of an inscribed plaque or slab.

The small, commemorative cairns differ in object from the identical piles of stones which crown almost every hilltop in the Highlands. Some of these were raised not so long ago by Sappers of the Royal Engineers, who piled them up in order to have sighting-points whilst engaged in making the Ordnance Survey. Others standing on the tops of hills and mountains, far away from any human dwelling, have accumulated through

8

countless centuries as each man of the rare visitors to the summit has added his stone to the heap. We still add our stones to the hilltop cairns and when we do it we are, quite possibly, perpetuating an age-old folk memory of worship in the high places.

In the Isles it is still the custom to raise a cairn at a place on the sea-shore where a drowned body has been washed to land—and there are very many tragic little piles of stones, dating back no longer than the last war when so many victims of submarine warfare found their last resting-place in a Hebridean Isle.

Obviously, the event that a cairn commemorates will only be remembered for so long as there is a continuing population to pass the story on. When the population dies out—or, as so often in the Highlands even today, is driven out—the story dies unless it is preserved by the written word.

One such cairn, whose tale is known by very few people, is that which stands beside General Wade's great road over the Corrieyarrick, leading from Badenoch into Lochaber. It is on the northern side of the road, about four miles into the hills beyond the recently emptied farmstead of Druimin or Melgarve. Nobody now lives in all the strath, which belongs to a large commercial firm, so that there are few people who know the story of the lonely cairn by the wayside. It is a tragic tale.

Late in the 18th century, a body of troops was marching from the King's House at Garv More *(see p. 156)* which was the staging-post between the garrisons at Ruthven-in-Badenoch and Fort Augustus, at the head of Loch Ness. Their march took place in the depth of winter and they were accompanied by a number of women and children, wives and families of soldiers stationed at Fort Augustus.

One of the women fell by the roadside and was unable to walk any father. It would have been equivalent to condemning a man to death from exposure to have left anyone with her at night and in the arctic conditions of a Highland winter. The troops had to march on and the woman had to be left behind.

On the following morning a search party was detailed to look for her and to bring her in. They found her lying dead but, to their amazement, they found her baby still alive in her bosom. They raised cairn where they had found her and then returned to their barracks, bringing the baby and the woman's body with them. According to tradition, the wife of the Governor of Fort Augustus, Lady Trapud, adopted the motherless infant.

There is an old Gaelic saying, *Cuiridh mi clach'nad charn,* which gives thanks for a kindness by returning the promise that it will always be remembered gratefully—a stone on the cairn of remembrance. The proverb still has a literal application—but the number who add a stone to the lonely cairn beneath the Corriyarrick are sadly few.

STONE BASIN AT TRUMPAN, *Isle of Skye.*
(O.S. Sheet 24: 235612)

THE CLEANSING WATERS

Ancient things always tend to attract legendary tales and when those things are in Celtic countries those tales naturally become embroidered and romanticised. Pooh-Bah, in *The Mikado*, epitomised the Gael's view of simple facts when he spoke of adding "corroborative detail to an otherwise bald and unconvincing narrative".

A stone basin, lying in the remote kirkyard of Trumpan, on Skye, possesses strange qualities which appear to be inexplicable and which, together with its position on consecrated ground, combine to give it a miracle-working reputation. For one thing, it never becomes dry.

Even in the hottest and driest summer, the basin still holds water and, according to local belief, the day when it finally dries out will mark *an Latha na Cruinne*, the Day of Judgment itself. Unkind sceptics suggest that the weather in Skye is never dry for long enough for the water to evaporate. That is as it may be! I prefer to believe the story and leave doubts to the disbelievers.

Other stones exist which have the power to draw moisture from the surrounding air and to condense it. One such stone is in England, built into the wall of a dungeon in Carlisle Castle—one of the most tragic stones in all the world, worn out into a smooth hollow, a few inches deep, by the tongues of hundreds of prisoners, confined without light, food or water, who sought to relieve their thirst by licking at the drops that condensed on the stone.

The basin at Trumpan may be similar to that in Carlisle. It is not the stone alone that possesses strange qualities, however. The water itself has extraordinary powers of cleansing and purifying objects placed in it

Visitors to the place frequently leave coins in the basin, which are removed from time to time and the money used for the upkeep of the site. What is odd is that, no matter how filthy the coin was when it was dropped into the water, within a day or two it will be found as bright as it was on the day that it was minted.

This actually happens and there is probably some scientific explanation of it. One hopes, though, that nobody will begin analysing and explaining the phenomenon, for it is always a delight to discover something that is unexplained and to credit it with being inexplicable. We lose a tremendous amount of simple pleasure when people explode mysteries.

The basin has a disputed origin. It may have served as a stoup for holy water in pre-Reformation days. It may, possibly, have served as a font. It may even have been a pagan stone, re-consecrated and applied to Christian uses when the Columban missionaries came to Skye from Iona.

What it used to be doesn't seem really to matter. What it is, though, is sufficient marvel. It produces water out of dryness and it purifies money that has been soaked in it.

KILPHEADAR CROSS *on North Uist.*
(O.S. Sheet 17: 725744)

THE MOTHER GODDESS

The cult of the Mother Goddess is one of the most ancient religions, in the West no less than in the East. It became depraved in some of its manifestations and was suppressed as other religions arose to supplant it. In spite of everything, though, it has never entirely died out and, even now, continues to exist in many unassuming ways.

It has survived in Britain in the legends which have been grafted on to the tales of many Christian saints. In particular, the tales of St Bride, or Bridget, bear witness to the firm hold which worship of the goddess of a similar name is still held amongst the Celtic peoples.

Some years ago a very primitive cross was unearthed in one of the oldest Christian graveyards on the island of North Uist. It was re-erected on a prominent hill as a memorial to a former minister of the parish.

Its stark simplicity shows that it far antedates the beautiful and elaborate crosses of the early Celtic Church, for its only ornamentation lies in the gently rounded breasts—fountain of early life—which rise from the surface of the stone.

We shall never know its origin. The cross was used as a symbol by religions that existed long before Christianity and, if this was a pagan cross, the fact would account for its having been hidden underground. It may, indeed, originally have stood as a simple representation of the Mother Goddess and was cut into a cross and used to mark the re-dedication of her shrine to Christian worship whilst, at the same time, bearing witness to the perpetuation of sanctity attaching to the site. It may even be an extremely primitive Christian carving, in which the sculptor embodied the age-old symbol of motherhood.

However it began, the cross stands as a most beautiful, simple and very moving relic; for in its strength and roughness there is a contrasting gentleness which is deeply emotional.

"MACBETH'S GRAVE" *Burial Mound near Belmont, Perthshire.*
(A.927)

BURIAL MOUNDS

From the very earliest times, our ancestors were buried with due regard for their requirements in a future life and, too, with some outward sign that should preserve their memory in future days. Their bodies were laid out ritually, frequently within a stone chamber, and with them were placed weapons, tools, articles of personal adornment, drinking vessels and even foodstuffs. Over all was raised an earthen mound (tumulus, barrow, tump—call it what you will) to mark the spot. It was left to the piety of later generations to preserve the name and the memory of the buried hero.

Individuals are still recalled in this way, in local memories. Notable is the long mound in Strath Ardle which covers the remains of the giant Pictish Prince who gave his name to the strath and whose grave lies close beside the road beyond Moulin and Pitlochry, in Perthshire.

Mounds were frequently placed prominently in order that they might be seen from a great distance, even though their size was comparatively small. An interesting example of such a tumulus is apparent from the A.9, a few miles north of Killicrankie and just south of Blair Atholl, where the burial mound stands exactly on the crest of a hill, silhouetted sharply against the skyline.

In Orkney, at Maeshowe, is a burial mound which stands no less than thirty-five feet high and which measures 120-feet in circumference. It contains a stone chamber which is entered through a 52-foot long passage. Like many other barrows, that of Maehsowe was used and re-used for burials, long after its first interment. Runic inscriptions here show that it was still used as a place of sepulture as late as 1150.

The tumulus illustrated here stands in a field near Belmont, the home of the great Liberal Prime Minister, Sir Henry Campbell-Bannerman. This, too, is in Perthshire and local traditions give two stories of its origin. One tale speaks of it as being the grave of a prince who was killed during the civil wars between Macbeth and Macduff. The other claims that it is the tomb of Macbeth, himself. Only excavation will prove the date of its origin. Probably it is far older than the days of Macbeth. That, though, is no reason for dismissing the local traditions in their entirety. The mound may well have been of ancient erection and have been re-opened and put to subsequent use for the burial of a hero, long after its original occupant had been forgotten.

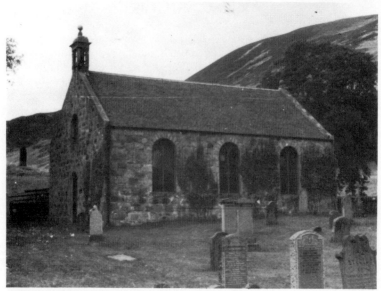

SPITAL OF GLENSHEE *(A. 93). Standing Stone on hillside beside the Kirk.*
(O.S. Sheet 49: 109703)

STANDING STONE
On the marches of Belmont Castle, South of Meigle, Perthshire.
(A.927)

STANDING STONES

Great monoliths are scattered all over the Scottish landscape—far more than are shown on the one-inch sheets of the Ordnance Survey maps. Most of them are relics of a dim, remote past. A few, though, have been erected in more recent days, following the traditional uses of prehistory.

Standing stones have marked sacred sites from times immemorial. The Book of Genesis (XXVIII, 18-22) tells of how Jacob raised a stone "for a pillar"—the same Stone as has long been believed to be that on which the Kings of Scotland have been crowned. The worship of "stocks and stones" was declared to be an abomination in Jewry.

Some authorities see these stones as phallic symbols, others give them a different interpretation. Whatever their original purpose, the fact remains clear that their use in places of worship and commemoration is both ancient and world-wide.

Through the centuries, many legends have become attached to the stones. Witches, wizards, heroes and kings are all alleged to have taken a part in raising them. Some are attributed to the Devil himself, as for example that which stands in the Ochil Hills, known as The Devil's Cradle, which brings strange and mysterious fortune to anyone bold enough to sleep on it at the turn of the year.

The majority of the stones are attributed vaguely to the Druids. This is certainly incorrect, for the stones were standing long before the Druids came to Scotland. However the story may be partially true, insofar as that ancient order of priesthood was accustomed to re-consecrate ancient places of worship and apply them to their own religious uses. To that extent, therefore, tradition may well stand on firm ground.

It is certainly true that the Christian Church did not scorn to use the hallowed sites of former worship. The church at Kingussie (A.9) stands on the site of a prehistoric stone circle, some of the stones of which are reputed to be incorporated in its foundations. At Spital of Glenshee, the great standing stone was left in position and, as is clear in the photograph, the church was built close beside it, showing that the early missionaries did not disdain to maintain continuity of worship in the places sanctified by earlier religions.

Some stones stand singly. Others are combined to form great circles and avenues, such as the wonderful collection of forty-eight stones at Callernish, near Stornoway, which dwarfs Stonehenge and remains one of the marvels of ancient Britain. Another stone circle stands beside the A.9 and is passed daily by hundreds of tourists, passing along the Great North Road and apparently more interested in reaching their journey's end than they are in seeing what lies on either side. This circle, only ten yards from the highway is immediately to the north of Ballinluig. (O.S. Sheet 49: 975535)—and there are many, many more, equally accessible and equally ignored by the passers-by.

Of the standing stones that have been erected in more recent times, Wade's Stone (see p. 138) has an interesting history. Most magnificent of all, though, is that which stands beside the road in the middle of Blair Atholl, in Perthshire (A.9). Rough-hewn, towering and grey, it bears the inscription of "1914 1918" and, with scarlet Flanders poppies at its foot, stands in noble dignity as a memorial of the men of the Atholl Highlanders who gave their lives in the Great War.

CELTIC CROSS. *Logierait Kirk-yard, Perthshire.*
(O.S. Sheet 49: 968520)

18

CELTIC ORNAMENTATION

Although it was generally absorbed into the Roman Church, the old Celtic faith left many relics of native art. Notably these are stone carvings, for stone is the most durable material. But sufficient manuscripts, brilliantly ornamented, survive to show us what a height of achievement was attained by the artists of nearly two thousand years ago.

Typical of Celtic decoration is the intertwined network which is either endless or, where a line comes to an end, has any free end 'protected' with a claw or a grotesque head. The dual idea appears to have been to symbolise eternity and, too, to guard against evil entering the symbol through a way that was unguarded. The crosses of Iona are famous, but there are many other similar works.

A charming Celtic Cross stands in the kirkyard of Logierait, in Perthshire. On one side it shows a splendid piece of carving, of the typical intertwined decoration. The other side shows the figure of a horseman who appears to be wearing the kilt—though this is most unlikely and what he is really wearing is a cloak or mantle.

THE RAM IN MOFFAT
A.701, A.708 and off A.74.
(O.S. Sheet 68)

20

THE MOFFAT RAM

Perched high on a cairn of massive rocks, the figure of a ram makes a splendid centre-piece to the market-place in **Moffat**.

Unfortunately, when I was passing through the town and stopped to photograph the statue, it was a quiet morning and there were only four people there, to whom I could apply for information regarding the ram—for there is no inscription on the base, just a fountain and trough for watering horses.

A small boy said, "Na! I've nae idea wha pit him there. D'ye see, though, he's deef? He's got nae lugs!" Fair enough, for if the ram has ears then they're so hidden under his fleece that they can't be seen.

Of the other three people, one was a stranger and knew nothing—nor did he appear particularly interested. One of the other two, however, said that the ram had been erected as a monument to the woollen industry which is so important to the South of Scotland. The third man broke in to say that it had been presented to the town by someone—he didn't know who—who had taken sheep from Moffat to Australia, or perhaps to New Zealand. He wasn't sure of that, either.

Most of my reference books say nothing of the ram, but wax lyrical over the properties of Moffat's waters. The few that mention the statue merely speak of it standing in the street, but fail to tell anything of how it came to be there or for what reason.

It is a magnificent and unusual monument—but who put it there, and for what purpose? I'll be grateful if someone will tell me.

EWAN MACLACHLAN'S MONUMENT
Fort William
(A.82. O.S. Sheet 46: 117748)

A BARD'S MEMORIAL

Eoghann Mac Lachuinn, Ewan MacLachlan, was born in Lochaber in 1775. His father was illiterate but was nevertheless held to be one of the most eloquent Gaelic orators in his time and, too, was esteemed as the finest of all tellers of old tales and poems.

Ewan determined that he would be a scholar and, with little leisure and less money, he drove himself to study. By his 21st year he had reached such a standard of scholarship as to attract the attention of Glengarry who supported the young man when he presented himself in Aberdeen as a candidate for a bursary. His competitors jeered at him on account of his rustic manners and his rude clothing—they changed their tone, though, when Ewan's name headed the list and he was declared to be chief bursar.

His university career was distinguished. On graduation he was presented with a Royal Bursary and, in 1800, he was given the appointments of Assistant Librarian of King's College and, at the same time, teacher of the Grammar School of Old Aberdeen. Later he was entrusted with preparing the Gaelic—English portion of the great, standard dictionary and he enriched this work with an amazing range of original research, comparing his native Gaelic with other Celtic tongues, with Greek and Latin—and even with examples from Hebrew, Arabic, Chaldean, Persian and other Eastern languages.

Considering all this, it is not surprising that Ewan killed himself with overwork and died, worn out by his toils, at the early age of 47.

Ewan MacLachlan won fame in the academic world but never allowed this to draw him apart from his own people. His Gaelic poems made him loved and respected throughout the Gaidhealtachd and today he holds a high place still amongst the bards.

In Aberdeen, his death was marked by unusual scenes as his body lay in state in the chapel of King's College where the Professors of both of Aberdeen's Universities, joined by the Magistrates of the city and by great crowds of students and of townsfolk, all gathered to honour his name. The great assembly formed a procession and, for several miles followed the hearse which carried his body homewards.

Ewan had directed that his body should be taken back to Lochaber, to be buried with his ancestors. On the long journey, his fame as a poet was demonstrated by the way in which, in every town and village, the people lined the road to pay a last tribute.

When the hearse arrived at Fort William, the crowds were so great that it was only with difficulty that the procession, now headed by Glengarry and a large number of his clansmen, was able to make its way through the streets.

Ewan MacLachlan was buried at Killievaodain, in Ardgour. A fine monument was raised to his memory and still stands in Fort William, but the town which once honoured him appears now to have forgotten him completely. The monument is notable for the neglect with which it is treated. The carved, Gaelic inscription is so weathered as to be almost illegible. The plaque which bears details of his death lies shattered at the foot of the plinth. Only the English inscription remains clear, with its exhortation to "The Sons of the Gael to follow his Footsteps".

Nobody seems to care . . . The sad fact is that Fort William is now largely populated by immigrants of an alien race from amongst whom came recently angry and arrogant protests against the "waste" of Inverness County rates in expenditure on voluntary classes in Gaelic.

THE UNICORN AT INVERKEITHING
In Fife, Inverkeithing Mercat Cross, sur-
mounted with a Unicorn. A few yards to
east of the A.90, in the middle of the
town.
(O.S. Sheet 62: 131831)

THE UNICORN OF SCOTLAND

The shield of our Sovereigns, since at latest the days of Alexander II, has been the "ruddy lion ramping in his field of tressured gold". The Royal Shield is supported armorially by Unicorns and these beasts have been held (though I do not know on what authority) to represent the Scottish nation and to remind the King of his peculiar status with regard to his subjects.

The point is that, in Scotland, the monarch is not entitled of his country, but of his nation. He is not King of Scotland but King of Scots—a very different thing as was shown clearly in the Declaration of Arbroath when even the Patriot King, Robert I, was warned that he ruled by will of the people who maintained the right to cast him out should he betray their interests. The Scottish King does not rule over his people, but governs with their support and by their consent.

The Unicorns which support the Royal Arms wear gold crowns around their necks as collars and, fastened to those crowns, each carries a 'leash' of chain terminating in a ring. The ring hangs free and is not fastened to the ground on which the Unicorns stand. This is held to symbolise the unfettered freedom of the Scots to support their King whilst maintaining the right to cast off a tyrant or a traitor.

It is just possible, I think, that the use of the Unicorn may have originated in the old name for Edinburgh, 'The Maiden Castle'. You see, a maiden provided the one and only way of catching wild unicorns. She had to sit in the forest where unicorns were known to wander and, after a while, one of the beasts would be sure to come close to her. It would watch her for a while and then would lie down, lay its head on her lap and immediately fall fast asleep. That gave the **hunters** their chance!

IN HADDINGTON
A.1, A.6093, A.6137, B6471.
(O.S. Sheet 63: 513739)

A MARKET-PLACE IN THE SOUTH

Scotland's close ties with France are demonstrated notably in the market-place of many towns in the South of the country. Kelso is an outstanding example and there are many others where, given brightly coloured shutters outside the windows, the town-centre could be exchanged for that of a French market-town and one would scarcely notice any difference.

Haddington provides an instance of this, apparent even in the photograph, which I took some years ago. Since then, the whole place has been splendidly restored and its 'Frenchiness' is now even more apparent. It is exactly like a French *place*.

The mercat cross in Haddington is a notable example of a Scottish town-cross—although it is not literally a cross, for it is surmounted by the town's emblem. Why, one wonders, did Haddington choose a goat? That animal is more usually associated with the Evil One than with douce burgesses!

LOUPING-ON STANE
Outside Duddingstone Kirkyard, by the Queen's Park in Edinburgh.

LOUPING-ON STANES

It isn't so very long since we depended upon the horse for all our transport, so it is hardly surprising to find reminders of this, scattered all over Scotland. Indeed, it would be remarkable if this wasn't the case, for, after all, horses have carried us and our belongings for centuries whilst the motor car has been here for little more than a single lifetime.

Most obvious of the reminders of horse-drawn traffic are the high, wide doorways that open into inn-yards, farm steadings and warehouses. We can see these in every village and town except, of course, for those which have been built in the last few years. There is no need to illustrate them, for we know them well and their size makes them very apparent.

Other relics of those former days are smaller and are easier to miss. One example is the protective stones which lean against the corners of walls, where buildings abut on the street. Sometimes, more rarely, old cannon barrels serve the same purpose, which was to save the buildings from being damaged by the iron-shod wheels of carts, driven too closely around the corner.

Short flights of stone steps, rising three or four feet high, stand in many market-places, outside kirks and beside the front doors of mansion houses. These are the louping-on-stanes, the mounting steps, by which a lady could place herself in the saddle without immodesty and a gentleman, old or inform, could mount his horse without having to swing himself up from the stirrup.

When next you see a louping-on-stane, take a closer look at the bottom step. Nine times out of ten, you will find that it is deeply worn—clear evidence of how many thousands of people have used it, during hundreds of years.

BUILDINGS

ROUND TOWER AT BRECHIN
Angus. A.94, A.935, A.933.
(O.S. Sheet 50: 596601)

Scotland's other Round Tower is
at **ABERNETHY,** *Perthshire. A.913.*
(O.S. Sheet 55: 190164)

ROUND TOWERS

The Viking raiders of the Scottish coasts, between the 9th and the 12th centuries, made churches and monastic establishments one of their first objectives because that was where they could expect to find gold and jewels amongst the Church vessels, votive offerings and vestments. The raiders possessed no artillery such as the old Roman *ballista* or catapult. Their only way of battering a way into a building was by improvising a ram from a heavy tree-trunk. The Celtic monks learned effectively to counter this sort of attack.

High, round towers were built, solid at their bases and with the doors high above the ground. No ram could be brought to bear on the doorway, which could only be reached by a ladder—and even then could only be entered one man at a time, because it was too narrow and to low to permit easy entry. If the ram was used against the base of the tower, it either bounced off the round wall or else was shattered against the stone. As for arrows—the windows were kept to a minimum, were small and placed so high as to be clear of all but the most fortunate of bowshots.

Only two round towers have survived in Scotland, although about eighty still stand in Ireland. Of the Scottish examples, the one at Brechin is the more notable. The walls are ninety feet high and the cap rises twenty feet higher still. The narrow door is six feet from the ground and the walls in which it is set are three-and-a-half feet thick. The doorway, moreover, is so constructed that no entrance could be forced by prising out its stones, one by one. Each stone around the entrance is a vast slab, as thick as the wall itself.

RIEVAULX ABBEY, *The West Riding, Yorkshire.*
Mother-House of Melrose. (B.1257.)

MOTHER OF MELROSE

People who like to declare that nothing good has ever come to Scotland from England could do far worse than travel southwards, to contemplate the massive ruins of Rievaulx Abbey in the hills of the North Riding of Yorkshire. From that Abbey came great and lasting good to the Northern Kingdom.

The original Abbey of Melrose had been founded at a very early date, long years before ever the Roman Church had penetrated into Scotland. In 687, after the death of St Cuthbert (and he was a Scot) his disciples brought his body to Melrose and it rested there until, finally, it was taken to Durham.

Eventually, the old Abbey fell into decay and, between the years 1136 and 1146, a new Abbey was built on a site farther up the Tweed. This was the Abbey whose ruins still stand, guarding the heart of King Robert I, the Bruce.

King David endowed Melrose richly and, in order that it should be well built, he invited monks to come from Rievaulx. A small community travelled northwards into Tweeddale to build their great Abbey, where they lived in great austerity, under the strict regulations of the Reformed Benedictine Rule of the Cistercian Order. Notably, the Cistercians were devoted farmers and it is to these immigrants from England that we owe all the original reclamation and agricultural development of the Tweed Valley.

Throughout its history as an Abbey, Melrose maintained close links with its mother-house of Rievaulx, in England. It is ironical, therefore, to know that it was the English who sacked and burned Melrose on no fewer than three occasions when both the English Kings Edward II and Richard II destroyed it to the best of their ability and, although it had been rebuilt spendidly after each occasion, it was finally ruined by the English invaders, under Hertford, in 1545.

What Hertford left undestroyed was wrecked, a few years later, by our own native iconoclasts of the Reformation, who received the full support of the citizens of Melrose whom for centuries, found the Abbey ruins a most convenient quarry.

I do not think that it is being unduly romantic to suggest that the prosperity of the Tweed Valley and its atmosphere of quiet peace both owe much to the work and, no less, to the prayers of those holy men who, six centuries ago, walked From England to settle in Melrose at the invitation of the King of Scots. And Rievaulx, too, whence Melrose received its birth, itself stands in ruins. *Tout passe, tout casse, tout lasse.*

ST KENNETH'S, KINLOCHLAGGAN. *A. 86.*
(O.S. Sheet 36: 536898)

SAINT KENNETH OF LAGGAN

Christianity came to the mainland of Scotland many, many years before ever St Augustine landed in England and the greatest of the early missionaries was Saint Columba, who travelled through the Highlands more than fourteen hundred years ago.

One of St Columba's companions, when he passed through Badenoch, was St Kenneth, his Pictish interpreter. Kenneth settled beside the great loch in Upper Badenoch and gave his name to the *lagan,* or 'dell', from which the whole, huge parish of Laggan was later to derive its title. The scene of his small sanctuary became one of the most revered shrines in all Celtic Scotland and, for many centuries, ranked second only to Iona in sanctity.

Scattered cairns on long-disused tracks, stretch for many miles over the hills of Badenoch, into Lochaber and far-off Argyll. They mark the roads taken by parties of bearers, bringing their kinsfolk to be buried.

Funeral processions would come from as far away as the Isles and each cairn marked a stopping-place, where fresh bearers would take over the bier from the former, wearied party.

The chapel fell into ruins and was rebuilt, as part of his penance, by Alain na Creach, the notorious Cameron freebooter. It stands back, some distance from the road to Loch Laggan, and is approached by way of the drive which leads to Aberarder Lodge. Many more people know of it by repute than have actually visited it, for the chapel of St Kenneth was the scene of the finding of the muskets of Neil Munro's great book, *The New Road.*

Now, in 1973, this ancient and sacred shrine is in almost complete ruin. Trees are growing through the loose walls, which they are demolishing foot by foot and year by year. The ruined lair, belonging to the Macphersons of Strathmashie, stands in the north-west corner. The few people who still live in this once thickly-populated district, remember stories of the chapel and will show you the grave of the factor who was cursed for evicting crofters and who was buried where grass will never grow. They will tell you, too, of the lovers who were parted by their parents and who eventually came to be buried on opposite sides of the chapel. Trees grew out of their graves and their branches intertwined above the roof, until a wretched man, inveighing against 'superstition', cut them down.

Little remains to show that this is one of the oldest and most sacred shrines in Scotland. A rough-hewn font stands in a niche beside the doorway. The kirkyard is filled with tombs, for both Protestant and Catholic favour still what little is left of the old enclosure, and both Faiths are buried here. Not only Scots lie beside St Kenneth's. The stones tell of people who have come from very far away, and the grave of a Newfoundlander speaks of a World War, which brought him back to the Old Country and to find his death here. No-one, however, appears willing to accept any responsibility for upkeep or for maintenance and, in a very few years, nothing will remain except the graves and a rickle of loose stones.

A few years ago, a small party of the Scots Patriots organisation spent some weeks of the summer holiday, clearing away some of the undergrowth and rebuilding something of the ruined walls. All credit to them! It is saddening that other, more wealthy bodies cannot be shamed into following their example—to say nothing of those private individuals who own the land and who, although living elsewhere, have surely a responsibility towards the land which they have acquired and towards what lies on that land.

INCHCOLM ABBEY. *In the Firth of Forth, reached by frequent motor-boat service from Aberdour. A.92.*
(Island—O.S. Sheet 62: 189827)

INCHCOLM

The history of the island of Inchcolm, in the Firth of Forth, goes back as far as the sixth century. It found fame, though, in 1123, when Alexander I was wrecked on the island but came safely to shore. In thanksgiving for his escape, the King established "ane nocht obscure monastar" which was dedicated to St Columba and which incorporated a little oratory which had been built by a Celtic monk during the Dark Ages and which still remains, slightly rebuilt in medieval times.

The Abbey, which was given to the Augustinians, was harried on many occasions by English fleets and the monks were often driven to seek refuge on the mainland. Nevertheless, its stout walls stood firm and, probably because of its isolated position, the Abbey escaped demolition by the Reformation mobs.

For nearly two centuries the island was used as a quarantine hospital, after the monastics had finally been depossessed. It was fortified during the Napoleonic wars and fresh batteries were installed during the Crimean war and both World Wars. It provided a burial-place for Canute's marauders, who were defeated by Macbeth and, centuries later, it provided the same service for sailors of the Tsar, when Nicolas I was permitted to use Inchcolm as a naval hospital, in 1845, when the Russian fleet lay in the Forth.

Despite the Reformation, which wrought such damage elsewhere in Scotland, the Abbey of Inchcolm still stands almost intact. If the monks who left it in the 16th century were to return today, they would see little difference.

Some damage has undoubtedly been done. It was done quite deliberately by the vandals of Edinburgh City Council who had bought the Abbey and commenced its demolition, intending to use its stones for the building of a municipal gaol. Fortunately, they found the medieval cement too hard to be loosened with any ease and they wearied of the work before it was too far advanced.

The Island and the Abbey are now under the care of the Ministry of Works. They may be visited at any time, and are well worth seeing.

Luffness (near Aberlady) A.198.

DOOCOTS

Doocots, which the English call 'pigeon-houses', were once a military necessity in Scotland and every possessor of baronial rights was required to build one and to maintain it. When an army of invasion marched northward from England, as happened only too often, a "scorched earth" policy was usually adopted. Crops were burned and, as far as was possible, cattle were driven off to a place of safety or, if this was impossible, they were slaughtered. The invaders were unable to live on the country, but it also meant that the defending garrisons ran the risk of starvation in the event of a siege. Pigeons, however, could not be destroyed nor driven off by a besieging army, nor was it possible to shut them in. Thus, the doocots provided emergency meat rations and it was doubtless as a precaution against siege and starvation that a whole tower in Rothesay Castle (Bute) was given over to the keeping of pigeons.

Even children were not exempt from the severe penalties which were ordained for illicit raiding of the doocots, and a law of 1513 decreed that a child who committed this crime should be *leschit, scurgit, and dung* (lashed, scourged and struck) *according to his falt.*

Clerical landowners were not exempt from the requirement to build doocots and a lease of one belonging to Cupar Abbey is still in existence, dating from 1473.

Pigeons were soon found to supply a valuable source of meat during the long months of winter. There was no known way of preserving meat, other than by salting it. All cattle, save only the breeding stock, were killed off each autumn and pigeons represented the only available supply of fresh meat. For the owners of the doocots, they provided meat that was cheap, too, because the birds fed themselves on the neighbours' products! The barons depended upon the meat of the pigeons for their winter food and the ownership of a doocot became a privilege, which was closely guarded. That the birds were fed and maintained upon the crops of the surrounding farmers was not considered.

In 1617 it was found that so many doocots had been built and the birds were so numerous that the crops were stripped over a large part of the country. A law was therefore enacted in an attempt to limit the ravages of the pigeons and the multitude of smaller landowners were forbidden to build doocots. Only a person holding lands of *a yeirly rental amounting to ten chalders of victual* was permitted to keep a pigeon house, and he was obliged to situate it within two miles of his residence.

Many of the doocots still stand. They are small, square buildings which visitors often mistake for the remains of castles. Naturally, they are not as plentiful as they used to be—at the end of the 18th century there were 360 of them recorded in the Kingdom of Fife alone—but those that still exist are frequently well populated with doos, who may well be descendants of the original inhabitants. They are worth looking out for, because they represent an interesting and important item in our history.

A notable example is the doocot at Auldearn (Nairnshire) where, in

Rothesay Castle, Isle of Bute

1645, Montrose raised his standard beside Boath doocot before the battle in which he decisively routed the army of the Covenanters. It is owned and maintained by the National Trust for Scotland. A small quibble here—if 'doocot' *must* be translated into English on the noticeboard, it is a pity that it is not done accurately. The Scots doo is not a dove. It is a pigeon.

Near Crail, Fife

ELGIN'S CHAPTER-HOUSE, *Moray.*
A.96, A.941, B.9012, B.9010.
(O.S. Sheet 29: 222632)

FAN-VAULTING IN THE CHAPTER-HOUSE

Elgin Cathedral was probably the most beautiful building ever to stand in Scotland—and it was one of the worst fated.

Built in 1224, in the reign of Alexander II, the cathedral was burned in 1390 by the infamous Wolf of Badenoch, a bastard son of Robert II, who had been ex-communicated for his misdeeds and thus took his revenge on the church. It was not until 1414 that its rebuilding was completed and then, less than a hundred years later, the great steeple collapsed under its own weight.

The main structure escaped the ravages of iconoclasts at the Reformation, but its eventual ruin was made certain when the Regent Moray ripped the lead from its roof and sold it in order to pay his troops.

The famous wooden panelling and carvings of its interior—as much as remained of them—were stripped from the walls and burned by an association of local ministers and barons, assisted by the rabble, in 1640. The steeple, which had been rebuilt after its original collapse, fell again in 1711 and, from then onwards, the cathedral served generations of Elgin burgesses as a quarry.

What still remains is beautiful in the extreme and none of the ruins show more loveliness than the remains of the Chapter House and the Prentice Aisle, of which latter a tale is told that is similar to the legend of the Prentice Pillar of Roslin.

Standing alone in the middle of the octagonal Chapter House is one slender, clustered pillar. From its head, like graceful branches, spring the fans of the vaulting which supports the roof, seemingly too slight and frail for the work that they have to do. The pillar's capital is carved with emblems of our Lord's Passion. It carries, too, the Royal Arms of Scotland and a shield which bears the chequer-board armorial bearings of the Stewarts, for it was a Bishop from that family who built the Chapter House.

Beauty stands everywhere in the Close of Elgin Cathedral. But no Scot, surely, can look at the beauty which survives without feeling shame at the pillage, ravage and sheer wanton destruction that have reduced a former glory to a mere shadow of its one-time splendour.

Scotstarvit, Fife. A.916

Castle Forter, Perthshire. B.951

"Z" FOR DEFENCE

All-round defence was an obvious necessity of medieval castles. The English achieved this, usually, by building circular turrets at each of the four corners of a central keep. England, though, was a far richer country than was Scotland and her barons could afford to build more elaborately than could the Scots and, after the building, they could also afford to man the castles with larger garrisons.

The peels and tower-houses of Scotland were built to a simpler design which was equally effective. They are best represented by the letter "Z", in which the central line shows the keep itself, and the two arms show two towers which projected from diagonally-opposite corners of the principal building.

Simple, rectangular peels were topped with steep roofs with the 'corbie-step' gables which are typical of all Scottish architecture, domestic as well as military. At the top of the walls and around the roof there was a 'cap', projecting beyond the line of the walls and running all around the keep. This was battlemented and provided a walk from which sentries could keep a look-out on the surrounding countryside and from which they could deliver missiles against any attackers.

Meanwhile, each of the two flanking-towers provided covering-fire along two sides of the building. In this way, one Scottish tower did the duty of two towers in the English design and, at the same time, allowed for the defence to be maintained with a correspondingly smaller garrison.

Examples of the "Z" castle are frequently to be seen, all over Scotland. Castle Forter in Glen Isla (road B.951) is close to the highway leading to Braemar and is a fine specimen. The illustration shows a later version of the design—Scotstarvit Tower, near Cupar in Fife (signpost on the A.916). Scheduled as an Ancient Monument and open to the public, this was built primarily as a laird's residence but, in the troubled times of the 16th century, it still retained most of the characteristics of earlier fortresses.

ROOF OF THE SPEED MAUSOLEUM. *(From inside, looking upwards.)*

THE SPEED MAUSOLEUM
Brechin Cathedral, Angus.
(O.S. Sheet 50: 596601)

THE OLDEST VAULTING

A few years ago, an inconspicuous little building stood beside the East end of Brechin Cathedral, in the graveyard which used to form part of the Cathedral Close. From the outside there was little to remark about the simple structure, it appeared to be no more than 'just another family tomb'.

Neither door nor gate closed the entrance and it was used as a repository for gardening tools. A beautifully engraved stone, against the wall, told that "This Isle or Tomb" had been built in 1797 by Robert Speed of Ardovie to cover the burying-ground of eight generations of his family, commencing in 1519.

Robert Speed was resentful. His family had, "past all memory", possessed the lands of Cruickton, in Kinnaird. Then, in 1519, his ancestor had exchanged them with Robert Carnegie of Kinnaird, who had given Kinnaird to him.

There is little extraordinary about this, for it was no more than a fairly usual family dedication, although there appears to be a certain amount of ill-will and rancour in its wording. Robert Speed quite evidently held a grievance against his forefather for that exchange of the family's lands—even though the deal had taken place two-and-a-half centuries earlier!

It was when the visitor looked upward that the unusual structure of the little building became apparent. The roof was neither arched nor yet was it normally vaulted. It was not supported by cross-beams nor by rafters. It was, in fact, built to a far earlier plan, which antedates vaulting by thousands of years.

In effect, the roof was made of large slabs of stone which, commencing at the walls, projected inwards with each succeeding layer slightly overlapping a few inches the one on which it was set. Lastly, when the gap had been reduced to a moderate size, the final sealing was accomplished with a single, large and heavy slab.

The roof was built to much the same plan as that which was used by our stone-age ancestors. It was effective. It was strong—and it marked a survival of building methods which must be almost unique.

**EDINBURGH—FORMER DWELLING HOUSES IN
PRINCES STREET**—*the back of Princes Street shops
glimpsed from Rose Street during reconstruction, 1965.*

THE LOST FACE OF EDINBURGH

Edinburgh's New Town was a magnificent piece of city-planning and is recognised as such all over the world and by everyone save, apparently, the City Corporation, whose members and committees have been, for some years, busily engaged in destroying all that, not so long ago, made Scotland's capital city unique. But of course, according to the Corporation, Edinburgh is not the capital any longer. By their advertising slogan they have proclaimed it to be "The Festival City by the Sea"—a sea whose water and shores they have so polluted with untreated sewage that where once we used to bathe we can, nowadays, not even walk to the water's edge without becoming fyled.

Some of the Corporation's plans for Edinburgh have, fortunately, been frustrated—a motorway through Charlotte Square, with the demolition of St George's Church, is one example. A car park in Queen Street Gardens is another. But we still have not heard the last of an urban motorway, spanning the Royal Mile near to the Palace of Holyroodhouse; and, we are told, the plans for a sky-scraper on the site of the Haymarket are still being considered. Meanwhile, in close association with the Universities of Edinburgh and Heriot Watt, the destruction of beauty goes happily on. George Square, once a haven of peace akin to an English cathedral close, has been hemmed in with rectangular towers and box-like concrete masses. The Grassmarket, offering great opportunities for re-building, has been walled in by an erection which looks like nothing so much as a gigantic public convenience. Looking northwards from the Meadows, the beautiful skyline of old Edinburgh has been destroyed. Southwards, from the Botanic Gardens and Howard Place, the entire horizon is blocked out by a vast block of cement. From Arthur's Seat, concrete rectangles dominate the view.

The New Town was designed and built for habitation and, as recently as thirty years ago, it still remained a place where people were born, grew up and lived. Now, unable to meet the huge rates demanded by the City Fathers, the whole life of the city has been torn out. The houses which were our homes are now offices. The mews, which held the stables and where cars could be garaged, have been pulled down or converted to commercial uses, whilst the beautiful streets are cluttered and defiled by rows—often double rows—of motor cars.

Princes Street was one of the first to lose its residential character, though, in place of the old homes, some notable buildings were erected. Almost everything that remained of architectural distinction has, in the past few years, been knocked down. There remain, however, one or two relics of its original character. One shop still retains the basement "area" which belonged to the dwelling house which originally stood on the site. Recently, another sign became evident during the demolition of houses in Rose Street, which runs behind Princes Street and parallel to it. Some of the modern shops in Princes Street were shown to be no more than facades and their backs were still those of the old living houses, unchanged in form although much altered in use.

51

PERTH.
One house restored **. . .**

DESTRUCTION IN PERTH

Three Roman roads met where Perth now stands and, according to
ancient legend, its original Kirk of the Holy Cross of St John the Baptist
—from which the city derived its medieval name of, St Johnstoun which
in modern days is preserved in the name of the local football club—was
founded at the beginning of the fifth century, fully a century before
St Columba landed on Iona and a good two hundred years before
St Augustine came to Canterbury. It is evident, therefore, that Perth
was a place of no small importance from very early times.

The earliest remains of ancient history in Perth were the two arched
chambers, with walls 3½-feet thick, which were part of a temple—demolished or buried by the late 1700s. The same fate has met almost all
medieval Perth which, in former days, was one of the glories of Scotland.
The Blackfriars, where Robert III's mother, Elizabeth Mhor, was buried
and where James I was murdered, has disappeared completely. So has
the Parliament Hall, where Scotland's Three Estates used to meet when
Perth was still the capital of the realm. The great Carthusian Monastery
has been demolished together with the tombs of James I and his Queen
and, too, of Queen Margaret Tudor, wife of James IV.

Gowrie House, scene of the mysterious attempt on the life of James
VI, was presented by an obsequious Burgh Council to the Butcher Duke
of Cumberland, in 1746. He sold it to the government, apparently despising the gift—as well he might. It was then turned into barracks, only
to be bought back again by the Council who sold it for a few hundred
pounds.

Cromwell, in his time, did plenty of damage to what little its own
citizens had left of the old city. It was left to the town itself, though, to
dispose of its mercat cross for a miserable five pounds because it inter-
fered with the traffic.

St John's Church, once defiled by the King of England who murdered
his brother, the Earl of Cornwall, on its altar steps, still stands, with at
least its venerable walls intact. It was, however, gutted at the Reformation. Later it was divided into three parts, patched and disfigured, until
at last it was in some part restored, by private subscription, as a memorial to the men of Perth who died in the Great War of 1914-18.

Although St John's Kirk retains the finest collection of pre-Reformation bells in all Britain—no fewer than eight of them—it is perhaps sym-
bolical that they are all silent.

Apart from the old Church, all that remains of ancient Perth is what
is commonly known as "The Fair Maid's House". Whether the Fair Maid
ever lived there, whether indeed there ever was a Fair Maid, are both
matters for conjecture. Scott, of course, told of her. But the trouble with
Scott's tales is that he tied his stories so closely with the fabric of actual
history that it is difficult to know where fiction ends and fact begins.

Scott certainly placed his Fair Maid in actual surroundings. Her father
was one of Perth's glovers, and the glovers were the most notable and wealthy
Guild in the city for many centuries. Her father's house is still standing,

... and the
remainder of a medieval city
replaced by plaques as a memorial
to vandalism.

in a back street, not far from the North Inch.

The ancient house was built some four centuries ago and remained in the possession of the Glovers' Incorporation until, in 1758, they sold it to Lord George Murray. They seem to have had second thoughts about the deal, however, for they bought it back again less than thirty years later. It belongs now to the Burgh Council, and it is virtually a new structure after having been completely rebuilt in 1895.

Having torn down all but two of its splendid and historic buildings, Perth saw a brief renaissance from 1795 until mid-Victorian days. Some notable pieces of architecture still survive, but one wonders how long it will be before they join medieval Perth in oblivion. Already a start has been made by the demolition of the house in which John Ruskin was brought up.

It is not inappropriate to remark that, despite the claims of our sister-kingdom, Ruskin was no Englishman. Brought up in Perth, he was educated at Edinburgh High School, was ashamed to own a grandmother from Croydon and was extremely proud of his Galloway ancestry. His enthusiasm for Scotland was accompanied by a considerable degree of Anglophobia which he frequently expressed as, for instance, in his *Praeterita*.

Perhaps, someday, the City of Perth will put a plaque on whatever wall is built where Ruskin lived, just as it has put plaques on the other modern and uninteresting successors to all that once was noble and historic.

We Scots are "geyan guid at the dingin' doun" and few of our towns are in any way blameless. If, however, this disgraceful national "sport" were ever to be laid open to competition, Perth would surely stand very high amongst the competitors.

18th CENTURY LINTEL
Huntly House in the Canongate, Edinburgh.

THE STONE ABOVE THE DOOR

Carved, stone lintels have been a notable feature of Scottish houses for many centuries. Some of the finest are still to be seen over the windows and doorways of our old palaces and castles, displaying the heraldic bearings of their original owners.

With the arrival of a powerful burgess class and, more especially when the Treaty of Union had put an end to Scotland's independence and her aristocracy and nobility tended to emigrate southwards, armorial designs became less common and we find less romantic demonstrations of the mason's art above the doors of the merchants' town houses.

Many houses of the 18th century, in the older towns and cities, show elaborate rebuses of the owners or builders. Others display elaborate initials, entwined in complicated monograms.

Many more proclaim moral texts and illustrations. The High Street and Canongate of Edinburgh boast a large number of such stones still on their original buildings. These, though, are only a fraction of the number which were displayed in former years. Casual demolitions and rebuildings have destroyed much that should have been preserved.

It is from one such house that the lintel in the illustration was taken. It lies, at present, against the wall in what used to be the garden of Huntly House in the Canongate, and it shows a man of the middle-classes, dressed in the costume of two centuries ago, giving a dole to a beggarman, whose wife and children stand expectantly behind him.

The stone bears the date 1759 and the text, "My Son defraud not the Poor of his living and Make not the Needy Eyes to wait Long. Ecc. iv. 1".

THE ARCHITECT AND THE COUNTRYSIDE
Aviemore, Inverness-shire, A.9.

THE MODERN ARCHITECT IN SCOTLAND

The humblest of older buildings fits comfortably into the landscape and the loftiest of ancient fortifications seems to blend with its surroundings. Even the most peculiar of Victorian Gothic and Baronial whimsies has a place in the countryside and seldom, if ever, has been allowed to clash with the natural scene. There are two evident reasons for their unobtrusiveness. The first is that they were designed to suit the life of the country and the second is that they were built with local materials.

Modern styles appear to take no account either of scene or of material. Stark, rectangular boxes, completely lacking in grace and designed regardless of the nature of their surroundings, they do not blend with the scene, but dominate it. Current architectural styles appear to take no account of anything save utility and produce nothing that is not regardless of the country and the country's tradition.

Long windows and heavy, horizontal lines are characteristic of the new buildings that are springing up in our cities. They weigh heavily on the eye, seeming to crush us beneath them—and one wonders just how much of "urban neurosis" may be blamed on the architects. An enlightening example of what I mean may be seen in Edinburgh where, at the juncture of George IV Bridge and the Lawnmarket, at the head of the Royal Mile, a new building has been erected by the Local Government Authorities. There, in a single glance, the viewer is oppressed under the horizontal masses of the new erection and, at the same time, lifted up by the tall elegance of the ancient buildings, whose vertical lines and tall gables raise a man's eyes upwards, freeing him from the claustrophobia that a modern design induces even in a wide street—and how much more in a street as narrow as those of medieval Edinburgh!

Edinburgh, it appears, will not be satisfied until the city has been made indistinguishable from New York, Tel Aviv or Johannesburg. When this has been achieved, people will begin to wonder why tourists no longer come to visit places where, a few years earlier, they had flocked. By that time, though, it will be too late to do anything about it.

Inverness has followed happily in Edinburgh's footsteps. Queen Mary's house has been demolished—and the City Fathers are proud of having preserved the cellars! Rectangular blocks have destroyed the beautiful vista which, a few years ago, was opened up to the green hill, crowned with its castellated 'folly'. Other towns have done the same and the infection has spread fast and widely. Cupar, for instance, has pulled down the old Parliament Hall—to make a car park. And so it goes on . . .

It is not only the cities and towns which are burdened with these monstrosities. The countryside, too, is being over-run by them. Witness the new hotel at Aviemore, in the heart of the Central Highlands, known locally as "the sair thumb". It would serve admirably as a design for a grain elevator on the Canadian prairie, but it surely has no place in the Highland scene. Or am I alone in feeling like this and am just too old-fashioned to appreciate modern trends?

THE BLACK BULL *at Moffat. A.701, A.708 and off A.74.*
(O.S. Sheet 68)

THE BLACK BULL INN

Moffat stands at the junction of the roads which lead from England to the two principal cities of Scotland, to Edinburgh and to Glasgow. Both have been highways along which droves passed southwards to the English markets during centuries and along which, too, carts loaded with manufactures and coaches with passengers have made their ways, north and south.

It is not surprising that Moffat required a hostelry for the stream of travellers, passing into and from England. It appears that an inn existed in the town at a very early date, under the management of monks from Melrose. It is not surprising, either, that the house which is reputed to be Moffat's oldest building is an inn, too.

When the Black Bull was built is uncertain, what is known is that its owner kept it as an inn in 1568 and that it has been an hotel ever since. It has, indeed, the reputation of being the oldest inn in Scotland—a claim which is disputed by several other establishments, though perhaps with not quite such solid grounds for their claims.

It was on a window of the Black Bull that Burns wrote his *Epigram on Miss Davies (On Being Asked Why She Had Been Formed So Small and Mrs A − − − So Big)*.

Ask why God made the gem so small
and why so huge the granite?
Because God meant mankind should set
That higher value on it.

The pane on which Burns wrote is believed to have been bought by one of the Tsars and taken to St Petersburg. Enquiries have been made of the Russian authorities but these have been fruitless. Probably the glass disappeared, as so much else did, at the time of the Revolution.

KINGS & QUEENS

QUEEN GUINEVERE'S TUMULUS
Meigle, Perthshire. A.94/A.927.

QUEEN GUINEVERE'S GRAVE

King Arthur's name attaches itself to an enormous number of places in Scotland and there are good, historical grounds for believing that he was an actual leader, not a character of romantic fiction, and that he was *dux bellorum,* a general officer in command of the armies of Cymric-speaking realms, fighting the Teutonic invaders during the fifth or sixth centuries, after the withdrawal of the Roman regular army. Similarly, there are sound arguments for believing that his great War of the Twelve Battles was fought in the old, Welsh-speaking lands which stretched across the country from Dunbarton to the Lothians.

Near Meigle, in Perthshire, Arthur's Stone and other names give evidence of an extension of the tales northward. Mordred, Arthur's nephew-son, is supposed to have occupied a fort whose remains may still be seen on the top of Barry Hill, nearby. In Meigle itself, outside the door of the church, is a mound which marks the traditional grave of Arthur's faithless consort, Guinevere. She is known, locally, as "the wicked Queen Vanora". This is acceptable, because "Van" (Gaelic *bhan*) is the exact equivalent of the Cymric *Guin,* meaning 'fair'.

In the auld wives' idiom, Guinevere "wis nae better than she shid hae been" and her unfaithfulness is remembered in the reputation which still clings to her grave. More than four centuries ago, the historian Boece recorded a belief, ancient in his time, that any young woman who walked over Guinevere's grave (he called her "Vanoria") would condemn herself to barrenness. The tale is still current in the district, for it is not long since I heard it declared, in all seriousness, that any young wife who sat or stamped on the mound of the wicked Queen would never bear a child.

The old school in Meigle contains a wonderful collection of ancient carved stones which were found in the neighbourhood. One of them, dating back into Pictish times, used to stand on Guinevere's grave. It shows a skirted figure surrounded by animals and was assumed locally to tell of the manner in which she was done to death.

Mordred, it is said, gave her refuge. One day, he came home to Barry after a day's hunting and found her misbehaving with a servant. Her punishment was to be torn to peices by wild animals (some say that she was trampled to death by horses).

Mordern archeologists, though, have put a different interpretation on the carving, (and I wish these people would keep quiet and refrain from spoiling a good story!). They say that the stone, which is at least a thousand years old, does not represent Guinevere and the wild animals, or horses. It shows Daniel in the lions' den.

Be that as it may, the fact that Guinevere's name and ill-repute should have been linked with the sculptured stone shows how strong and how ancient is the tradition which ties her to the place.

EILEAN NA RIGH and ARDVERIKIE, *Loch Laggan. (A.86).*
(O.S. Sheet 36: 499876 and 492858)

A SEAT OF ANCIENT KINGS

It is thirteen hundred years since St Kenneth came to the head of what is now known as Loch Laggan and he found a flourishing small community living there. Amongst them he built his church, which eventually became one of the most sacred shrines in all Scotland, ranking next in sanctity to Iona itself. Now the district is almost empty, after these many centuries of habitation. It is becoming even emptier, too, as year by year more and more people leave. For this fact the neglectfulness of absentee landlords and the 'sporting interests' of large commercial concerns must surely bear much of the responsibility.

Kinlochlaggan has a royal as well as a saintly history. Queen Victoria is reputed to have contemplated making her Highland home at Adverikie on Loch Laggan-side. However she is said to have found the Badenoch midges too aggressive and, instead of Strathmashie, she chose to live at Balmoral on Deeside.

Royalty, though, found its way here long before Queen Victoria. In the days when the Scots were still under pressure from the Pictish kingdom, when the seat of government was at Dunkeld, the Kings of the Scots had a residence on an island in the loch. There are believed to be no fewer than seven of these kings, lying buried beside the hill on which they used to raise their banner. This is the origin of the name, *Ard Mheirighidh* (anglice, Ardverikie) which means, The Hill of the Standard.

Two islands lie in the loch, under the shadow of Ardverikie. On the larger of the two can still be seen the remains of ancient walls, made of unhewn stones set in mortar. *Eilean nan Righ*–The King's Isle–is its name. King Fergus is attributed with the first building here. A short distance away lies the smaller island, *Eilean na Coin*–the Isle of the Hounds. Here the old kings kennelled their hunting dogs. The names, the tumuli and the footings of the walls–nothing else remains to tell of the playground of monarchs in days long past.

ALEXANDER III's MEMORIAL
*Near Kinghorn, Fife. Two miles
eastwards from Burntisland. A.92.*
(O.S. Sheet 56)

THE DEATH OF A KING AND THE END OF AN ERA

Whan Aleisander oor King was dede,
That Scotlaunde led in luve and le,
Awaie was wealth of ale and brede,
Of wyne and wax, of gamyn and gle . . .

In all history it can have seldom occurred—if ever—that the death of one man brought more distress to his country than did that of Alexander III to Scotland in 1286. His only heir was his infant grand-daughter, Margaret of Norway, who died before she had ever seen what would have been her kingdom. Immediately followed the interim period when the Guardians were appointed to govern the country until the nearest heir should be discovered. Soon the realm was split between rival claimants to the throne and Edward I of England, supposed to be an honest man and ruler of a friendly kingdom, was invited to arbitrate.

Edward's ideas of arbitration were those of Hitler. His armies marched into Scotland in blatant, open aggression, launching a war that was to continue for three hundred years. The immediate result of this ill-faith was that a newly-united nation was split threefold; into the groups of Patriots, those of the English supporters and, too, into the division between Celtic North and Anglicised South and East. Seven centuries later, Scotland suffers from these same divisions.

Alexander ruled for thirty-seven years and, during his long reign, he achieved victories in peace which were no less notable than those which he won in combat. He put an end to Norse claims upon Western Scotland by a decisive victory at Largs. He imposed a rule of impartial justice upon a turbulent people. He travelled all over his realm and united the entire nation under his personal leadership.

One of Alexander's greatest achievements was that he gave a formula to Scotland's nationhood and successfully maintained his country's rights against England's threats. So it was that he declared proudly to England's King, 'No-one save God alone has any right to homage for my Kingdom of Scotland, nor do I hold it of anyone save of God.' Later he added, 'I do homage to you (the King of England) only for such lands as I own in England.'

All was brought to nothing when, on a stormy night in March, his horse plunged over the cliff at Kinghorn, in Fife. Despite the efforts of the patriots, the country fell into anarchy and ultimately, for a while, under English rule. A new party arose in Scotland—one which still is with us—of men who sought advancement from the South, despising the culture and traditions of their own nation. The Gaelic element in the country withdrew itself into the hills of central and northern Scotland and to the Western Isles. The realm was split permanently.

Oure gold was changyd in to lede.
Cryst, borne in the Vyrgynytie,
Succoure Scotland and remede
That stad is in perlexytie.

Six centuries after the tragedy, a monument was erected near the place of the King's death. It stands beside the A.92 highway, between Kirkcaldy and Burntisland. Few passers appear to notice it—and even fewer stop to examine it and to consider all that it represents.

Robert the Bruce, King of Scots.
Dr Pilkington Jackson's great
statue on the field of Bannockburn.
(A 80 South of Stirling.)

King Edward I of England and
Queen Eleanor. Statues at Lincoln
Cathedral.

TWO KINGS—ROBERT I AND EDWARD I

A man whom one nation accounts to be a hero is often regarded in a very different light when seen from the view-point of a neighbouring realm. Thus, King Robert I, King of Scots and Edward I, King of England, contemporaries of each other, bear widely differing characters which depend entirely upon whether they are viewed from the north or the south bank of the Tweed.

We in Scotland look upon Robert I, the Bruce, as the great patriot king who regained our independence and who re-established Scotland as a free member of the community of nations. We see his campaigns into England as being normal military operations whereby he followed up his victories on the battlefield by taking the war into enemy territory. So it comes as something of a surprise to read a very different account of those same campaigns, written by English historians. King Robert's invasion of England and his capture of the Hartlepools are described as forming part of a savage and unprovoked attack upon a defenceless people upon whom he inflicted all the horrors of looting, rape, plundering and slaughter. Ah, well! We can remember that Alice saw things very strangely, too, when she found herself on the other side of the looking-glass!

No contemporary portrait exists of Robert I. Probably the finest representation of him which we will ever have is that shown in the great statue at Bannockburn, in which his features were modelled upon a cast of the king's actual skull.

Edward I of England, his great enemy, can still be seen as he was portrayed by an artist of his own time. The Scots nicknamed him 'Longshanks' in derision. In his own kingdom, however, he elected to be known as *Malleus Scotorum,* Hammer of the Scots—a title which remains engraved upon his tomb in Westminster Abbey.

King Edward's statue stands in a niche on the walls of Lincoln Cathedral, where he is accompanied by his first wife who seems to have been quite a good looking lady. His second wife stands nearby, but she was out of range of the camera—and this was unfortunate because, if the sculptor was in any way accurate, she was a lady who would have taken prizes at any modern beauty contest!

A ROYAL STEWART'S GRAVE IN ENGLAND
"The Quaker Princess" at Wisbech, Cambridgeshire.
(A.47/A.1101.)

A SCOTS KING'S QUAKER DAUGHTER

Late in the year 1688, King James VII (James II in England) had left his two kingdoms, the Great Seal had been thrown into the Thames and his daughter had succeeded under the title of Mary II, to share the thrones with William II (IIIrd of England) whom she had married. The so-called "glorious" revolution had been completed and, inconspicuous and almost unnoticed, a little Quaker lady sat on the bridge at Wisbech, in East Anglia, offering her services as a casual worker to farmers. This small, demure lady was Jane Stewart, daughter (albeit illegitimate) of James VII and II, who had for many years been a high favourite at Court and who now, at the age of 34, had found obscurity, shelter and refuge in a small Cambridgeshire market-town.

Jane Stewart was born in 1654 when her father and his brother, Charles II, were living at the French Court, exiles from Cromwell's dictatorship. There does not appear to be any record of her mother's name and all that is known of her is that she was a member of the French Royal entourage. What is certain is that James, then Duke of York,

74

accepted her openly as being his daughter and, both in exile and in Whitehall, after the Restoration, she was a bright and popular member of the Court.

It was while she was living in Whitehall that her father sent her to travel in Europe and to visit her cousin Elizabeth, "The Winter Queen" of Bohemia, at whose court many Quaker refugees from religious tyranny had found an assured welcome. It must have been there that she made her first acquaintance with the Society of Friends and, after her return to London, she continued to meet with its Members. It appears that she actually joined them and fell in love with a young Quaker—his name is not recorded—and determined to marry him.

All arrangements for the marriage had been completed—but none took place. Jane set out for the Meeting House on what was to have been her wedding day, travelling in a coach together with her intended husband and his brother. Someone waved a cloth by the roadside and the horses bolted. The coach was overturned and shattered. Jane's bridegroom was killed on the spot.

At the Revolution, Jane took refuge amongst the Friends of her adopted faith in Wisbech. Her associates must have known who she was, because nothing ever remains quite secret in a small community, but they accepted her quietly, after the Quaker manner, to live in their midst as one of themselves.

The even course of her life was only twice broken—and on both occasions the interruption came from Scotland.

The first instance was when a coach, bearing the gyronny cross and lymphad of Argyll on its panels, appeared in Wisbech. Jane hid herself, fearing that it was intended to take her to London, to be imprisoned or sent into exile. No search was made for her, however, and she emerged once again to resume her everyday life.

On the second occasion, she left Wisbech and travelled to Scotland to meet her half-brother, the *de jure* King James VIII and III, who had landed in the fateful year of the Fifteen. They met once before the Rising collapsed, when the Stewart King returned to his exile in France and Jane to her home is Wisbech.

With only these two interruptions to her peaceful life, she lived to the age of 88—a notable achievement in the eighteenth century. She died in Wisbech and was buried in the plot behind the Quakers' Meeting House. Her grave is outlined with a low, closely-trimmed box hedge and is marked in miniature topiary with "J S – 88 – 1742". Recently a headstone has been added with the inscription, "Jane Stuart – Died – 1742 – Aged 88 years".

Jane's simple grave is fitting to the simplicity of her Quaker life. It is looked after with loving care, for the people of Wisbech still keep affectionate memories of their "Quaker Princess". It is a heart-warming experience for any Scotsman to discover, in England, this evidence of love for a long-descended daughter of our own Royal Family, of whom hardly anyone has any knowledge, here in the land whence her forefathers came to rule over the Southern Kingdom.

JACOBITES

Lady Grange's Tombstone at Trumpan, Skye.
(O.S. Sheet 24: 235612)

A JACOBITE SCOUNDREL

Sentimentalists and lovers of romance like to believe that all supporters of the exiled Stewarts were paragons of virtue and of loyalty. This, however, was far from being the case and the Jacobites had as great a proportion of rogues amongst them as did their opponents.

One outstanding villain was Lord Grange, living in Edinburgh, who was described by Dr Alexander Carlisle as being one of those who "passed their time in alternate scenes of exercises of religion and debauchery; spending their days in prayer and pious meditation, and their nights in lewdness and revelling". Even after making the fullest allowances for stern Presbyterian prejudice, this description holds good. Lord Grange was indeed a shocking character. He was a Whig, yet he intrigued with the Jacobite Tories. He professed sanctity, yet he was one of the most debauched men in an age of debauchery.

In 1732, Lord Grange either believed or else persuaded himself to believe that his wife had overheard some of his plotting with a party of Jacobite conspirators. She was a feather-headed little woman and he feared that her gossiping tongue might give him away. Accordingly, he took measures to get rid of her and, as a first step towards that end, he announced that she had died suddenly, and immediately, with a great public display of mourning, he pretended to bury her.

Lady Grange was far from being dead. Men, in her husband's pay, had taken her by force to the North of Scotland and had shipped her over to St Kilda. There she was held in such close and rigorous confinement that she lost her reason altogether. She died, insane, in 1749, after seventeen years of incarceration.

Even after death, she was not spared indignity. Her coffin was shipped to Skye, but Grange feared lest news of her funeral should become known and be the cause of a public demonstration. Accordingly he gave ceremonial burial, for the second time, to a coffin that was filled with nothing else than stones. At the same time, he caused his wife's body to be smuggled to a lonely kirkyard in the north-west corner of the island and buried her there, in dead secrecy, near Vaternish Point.

Many years passed before Lady Grange's grave was marked in any way. A carved stone stands at its head, now, bearing mute memorial to one of the most shocking tales of villainy in all Scottish history. The inscription, covered with lichen but still legible, is simple. It reads, R.I.P. – Rachel – wife of – The Hon. James Erskine – Lord Grange – Died Aug. 1749".

THE CROSS AT LEEK, *Stafford-shire. A.523/A.520/A.53.*

JACOBITE CANNON AT SEDBERGH, *West Riding. In Back Lane, off A.684.*

JACOBITE MEMORIES IN ENGLAND

At Leek, in Staffordshire, Prince Charles Edward slept in the vicarage and his bodyguard spent the night of December 3rd, 1745, in the village. They were described as being "likely men" whose uniform was "blue, faced with red, and scarlet waistcoats with gold lace"—which sounds somewhat different from the tale that the Jacobite army consisted only of ragged savages from the remote mountains.

Local inhabitants show marks on the shaft of the Saxon cross, which stands between the vicarage and the church. These, they maintain, are the scars of bullets fired by the Highlanders, who used the cross for target-practice. To anyone with knowledge of the religious feelings of the Jacobite army, the story sounds unlikely—to say the least of it. The people of Leek, however, insist upon its truth and are still inclined to look askance upon visiting Scotsmen, just in case they may meditate further assault upon the historic relics in their town!

At Sedbergh, in the West Riding of Yorkshire, three cannons stand at different places by the roadside. They are reputed to have been left behind by the Jacobite army during its retreat. Sedbergh, however, lies a good few miles away from the road taken by the Prince's army and one wonders how these fairly heavy pieces of ordnance found their way so far.

It may be that the cannon are relics not of the Forty-five but of the previous Rising, the Fifteen. Be that as it may, the cannon are there in Sedbergh and the local tradition is firm on the point that they were left by the Jacobites. Indeed, it is hard to imagine who else could have been in that area, bringing artillery with them.

We may assume that these guns were indeed left by supporters of the exiled Stewarts. Who the men were, though, and when they left the cannon there—indeed, how they came to be so far from the road which the army followed—is something upon which tradition remains silent.

GLENSHIEL. *A.87.*
(O.S. Sheet 35: 9911 33)

GLENSHIEL

The Jacobite Rising of 1719 passes almost unnoticed in these days.
Yet of all the Risings, the 'Nineteen' was the one which started with
greatest chance of success—and which failed most completely.

Spain was at war with Hanoverian England and James VIII was
invited to assist. Ormonde was already in Cadiz, a huge fleet was assem-
bled under his leadership. 5000 trained soldiers, 10 field pieces and arms
for 15,000 were embarked in twenty-nine warships. In addition, the
Earl Marischal was entrusted with another force which consisted of
three frigates, with six companies of infantry aboard them, and a large
supply of arms and ammunition for Scottish loyalists.

James, through no fault of his own, was delayed until after the fleet
had sailed—and that was his good fortune, for the ships ran into a fort-
night of gales and was irrevocably scattered.

The Earl Marischal's smaller force, though, had sailed earlier and had
missed the gales. It landed on Lewis and was soon joined by a noble
company of refugees, including many whose names were to become
famous in the Forty-five. Hardly had the little army come ashore,
though, than it was struck by the trouble which seems to arise always

from the Scottish temperament. The two leaders disagreed and refused to be reconciled. The Earl Marischal held the exiled King's commission to lead the expedition, but the Marquis of Tullibardine suddenly produced a commission which James had granted him two years earlier, for an expedition which never took place. He now claimed seniority, by virtue of his earlier orders. Chaos resulted.

The leaders parted and made separate camps. The Earl Marischal captured the castle of Eilean Donan, where he disembarked all the arms and ammunition and he then sent the frigates back to Spain lest they should be of use to Tullibardine. A few days later, a small squadron re-took the castle and captured every man and all the stores that were inside.

On the mainland, the Spanish troops were joined by about 1,000 Highlanders. They were attacked in Glenshiel by a force under General Wightman—the same officer who had been defeated at Sheriffmuir four years before. The Highlanders faded away after no more than a token resistance. The Spaniards retreated up the pass which is still known as *Bealach na Spainteachan,* the Pass of the Spaniards, and there they surrendered. Hardly any casualties were inflicted on either side. The Spanish prisoners were sent to Edinburgh and were repatriated three months later.

The Nineteen was over, almost before it had begun. And yet, with united leadership and with different weather, it might so easily have been successful.

In Glenshiel, a few years ago, I was shown the pool in the river where the fleeing Jacobites threw away their arms. If my informant was correct, the weapons are still there. I have no reason for doubting that his memory of past days is completely sound. He took me farther down the glen and, a short distance from the road, he showed me a large boulder which, he said, was called *Clach na Dochdair,* the Stone of the Doctor.

Naturally, I asked him who the doctor had been, that he should be remembered in this way. My friend told me. *"Fada, fada roimh so,"* he started, in the way that so many Gaelic tales begin. A long, long time ago, an English doctor came here and he had very bad manners. They say that he ate his meal, sheltering behind that stone.

Scholarship is not uncommon in the Highlands, but bad manners are extremely rare. So it is that Dr Johnston left his memory behind in Glenshiel, not by his wisdom but simply on account of his boorishness!

Donald Fraser's Anvil at Moy Hall, Inverness-shire. A.9.

THE ROUT OF MOY

The Rout of Moy is one of the least-known battles of the Forty-five—possibly because there were very few casualties. It is none-the-less notable, for two reasons. It was an occasion when five men successfully routed seventy of their enemy and it was the victory which ended the unbroken record of success which, until Culloden, had been maintained by the Jacobite army, in retreat as well as in advance.

Norman Macleod of Macleod, Chief of his Clan, was a supporter of the Hanoverian Government. His clansmen, however, were mainly sympathisers of the Jacobite cause. The Chief allowed his men to believe that he intended to lead them to join Prince Charles's army on the mainland and so was able to bring a reasonably large force with him when he came over from Skye in the Spring of 1746. With them was Macleod's own piper, who was none other than Domhnuil bàn, one of the greatest of all the great MacCrimmons and a man who was devoted to the House of Stewart.

Wearing the Jacobites' White Cockade, the Macleods marched through Glenmoriston, where they came into contact with the Hanoverian troops under Lord Loudoun and, at last learning of their destination, were issued with Black Cockades.

Lord Loudoun had received intelligence that the Prince was staying at Moy, residence of the Mackintosh, some eleven miles south of Inverness. He at once led his force out, to attempt a capture, and he ordered the Macleods to go ahead as an advance party, to effect a surprise attack.

News travels both ways, and information of the forthcoming attack came through to Moy. It arrived too late, though, for a proper defence to be organised. Lady Mackintosh, whose staunch support of the Jacobite Cause combined with her keen presence of mind to bring her the nickname of "Colonel Anne", took what steps she could, instructing Donald Fraser, the local blacksmith, to see what he could do to effect a diversion.

Donald collected four other men and the five took up positions on the hillside, widely separated from each other and hiding behind peatstacks. As the Macleods approached, they received a similar welcome to that which Gideon accorded the Midianites. The five defenders fired off their muskets, running from place to place between shots, to give the impression of a large number of marksmen. They lit small fires, shouting to imaginary forces of Macdonalds and Camerons to attack on all sides and to give no quarter.

Night had fallen and the Macleods, bewildered by the darkness, were even more bewildered by a thunderstorm which suddenly broke out and make the night even more terrifying. MacCrimmon, the supporter of the Stewarts, was, ironically, killed by the first shot to be fired, another man was wounded and the Macleods fled, "halling the pyper after them till they got a horse and cart to carrie him of". They did not halt until they reached Inverness.

The heroic blacksmith was thereafter given the title of *Caiptein nan Coig,* Captain of the Five, and his anvil is still preserved amongst the Clan Chattan treasures and relics in the possession of Mackintosh of Macintosh, at Moy Hall.

CULLODEN MEDAL
Writer's Collection. *(In the Clan Macpherson Museum, Newtonmore – on loan.)*

SWEET WILLIAM OR STINKING BILLY

Scottish history appears to lend itself to romantic treatment and to sentimentality which is at times mawkish, cloying and completely inaccurate in its affectations and inventions. The story of the Forty-five has suffered from this more than any other chapter in our country's tale and it is sometimes salutary for us to consider the facts which novelists and starry-eyed dreamers usually try to forget or to ignore.

Even the Highlanders were not united in their support of the Jacobite Cause and, in the civil war of 1745/6, there were as many Clans supporting the Hanoverian dynasty, either in the army or else biding at home, as there were in arms under Prince Charles Edward, Regent for his father, the *de jure* King James VIII and III.

In the Lowlands of Scotland and in England, too, many thousands of professed Jacobites found a thrill in meeting by candlelight and toasting, "The King over the water". There were precious few of them, in either country, who were prepared to take the sword to support their loyalty to the old dynasty. Even amongst the Scottish regiments of the Jacobite army, the loyalty of the officers was not completely devoted to the Stewarts but was inspired by patriotic notions. Not everyone had welcomed the Treaty of 1707 which had abolished England and Scotland, uniting them into the new entity of Great Britain. More than a few broadswords, drawn for King James, were engraved with, "No Union" and similar mottos.

In 1746, mourning was confined mainly to the glens of the north— where ironically, the Clans who had been loyal to King George were made to suffer as sadly as those who had risen against him. Over the rest of the United Kingdom, celebrations of victory over "rebellion" were widespread. When, after Culloden, the bells rang out in London, they rang no less merrily in Glasgow.

The Culloden commemorative medal, here illustrated, is from the writer's own collection and was given to him a few years ago in Canada, whence it had found its way. It was struck in London and it shows the "Butcher" Duke of Cumberland, triumphantly mounted and in his glory. The reverse bears a battle-scene with the date of the battle and the legend, "Rebellion Justly Rewarded".

In the South, people honoured the Duke by naming a flower after him, Sweet William. In the North, where his memory is still held in abhorrence, a noisome weed was called Stinking Billy.

Personalities and characters, no less than historical facts, look very different when viewed from opposite sides of the fence!

THE CLUNY EPERGNE
Clan Macpherson Museum, Newtonmore, Inverness-shire. A.9.

THE HUNTED CHIEF

Ewan Macpherson of Cluny, remembered as "Cluny of the Forty-five", was a notable leader in the Loyalist army and, after Culloden, was accorded the distinction of being valued at 1000 guineas, "dead or alive", by decree of 'Butcher' Cumberland. In spite of the enormous temptation that this presented, Cluny lived in his own home-country of **Badenoch** for years and nobody came forward to betray him, although he was near to to capture on several occasions.

One such incident occurred when he was living in the house of Dal-chully, in Upper Strathspey, where there was a secret room (destroyed by a later owner of the house) in which he could hide if emergency arose. Sir Hector Munro, however, was too quick for Cluny. He had the area surrounded by a force of cavalry and, with a troop of horse, rode up to the house and ordered everyone to come out. Cluny had no time to dive for cover in his room but, quickly, he put on a servant's coat and walked casually round to the front of the house where he offered to hold Munro's charger for him.

When the officer came back, after a fruitless search, Cluny helped him to mount. As he gained the saddle, Sir Hector turned to his volun-teer horse-holder and asked him, "Have you seen Cluny Macpherson?"

"No, I have not," was the answer, "and if I had seen him, I would not tell you!"

"I don't believe you would," Sir Hector said. "You're a fine fellow—and here's a shilling for you."

No portrait exists of Cluny of the Forty-five, but his grandson, known affectionately as "Old Cluny" was said to bear a very close resemblance to him. It was fitting, therefore, that "Old Cluny", as a young man, should have been taken as model for the figure of the Highlander in the great epergne which his Clansmen presented to Old Cluny at his golden wedding in 1882—the subject of the work being his grandfather's meeting with Sir Hugh Munro.

The epergne was the work of Clark Stanton, A.R.S.A., and is esteemed one of the finest examples of a silversmith's craft, anywhere in Europe. It is now the property of the Clan Macpherson Association.

Together with the representation of Cluny receiving his 'tip' from Sir Hector, the Association also shows an interesting example of the shilling that was minted in 1745, which may well be a type of the coin which was given to the Chief. *(See page 90).*

THE 'LIMA' SHILLING OF 1745

THE SHILLING OF 1745

When Cluny Macpherson was given a shilling by Sir Hector Munro, in 1746, (*The Hunted Chief*) the coin was, in all likelihood, that which had been minted to a unique design during the first year of the Rising, in 1745, when shillings were struck to commemorate the notable achievement of the previous year when, in 1744, Admiral Anson returned to the United Kingdom at the end of his three-year voyage around the world.

During his long circumnavigation, Anson accumulated a vast amount of bullion, valued at more than half-a-million pounds—representing several millions in modern value. Much had been taken from the Spanish treasure-ship *Nuestra Senora de Covadonga,* which the Admiral had intercepted on her voyage between Mexico and the Philipines.

The treasure consisted mainly of Spanish-American silver coins, though there was a quantity of gold amongst it, too. The entire booty was sent to the Royal Mint and it was decided that the occasion merited the issue of a special coin, to mark the occasion. A new shilling was designed, on which the word 'Lima' was shown, beneath the King's effigy, to serve as a provenance mark, giving honour to Anson's exploits at that port.

The armorial device on the reverse of the Anson shilling is complicated. Four shields are those of England and Scotland combined, of Ireland, of France and of Hanover—the latter being an intricate affair showing two leopards (Brunswick), a rampant lion (Luneburg), a white horse (Hanover) and, over all, 'an escutcheon of pretence' bearing the Imperial Crown of Charlemagne.

The initials which surround the shields show the fantastic titles claimed by the early Hanoverian Kings. "M.B.F. et H. REX F.D.B. et L.D.S.R.I.A.T. et E." King of Great Britain, France and Ireland. Defender of the Faith. Duke of Brunswick and Luneburg. Arch-Treasurer and Elector of the Holy Roman Empire. What a fanfare of trumpets for a wee, wee Gairman Lairdie, who was so soon to pack his bags in fear lest his cousin should regain the British throne!

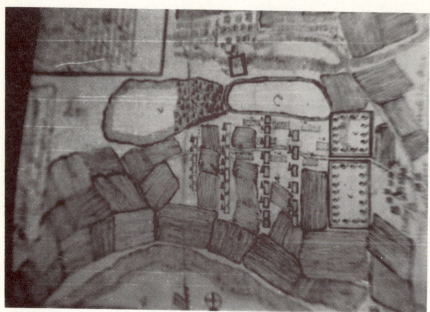

The Battlefield of Prestonpans

The Battle of Culloden
Pages from the Memoirs of the Chevalier Johnstone
(Clan Macpherson Museum, Newtonmore)

THE CHEVALIER JOHNSTONE

The Chevalier Johnstone was the mildly dissipated son of an 18th century Edinburgh lawyer and was brother-in-law of Lord Rollo. As a young man, he had been sent to Russia by his parents in the hope that foreign residence might cure him of his bad habits. It was not long, however, before he came home again and resumed much the same life as he had led before.

His religion was Episcopalian which led him, almost automatically, to being Jacobite in politics. In 1745 he was amongst the few gentlemen in Southern Scotland who showed the courage of their convictions by joining the forces of the Rising. He was appointed A.D.C. to Lord George Murray and, later, he became assistant A.D.C. to the Prince, himself. He held his appointment until the victory at Prestonpans, after which he raised a company of troops for the Royal Service and, with the rank of captain, was enrolled in the Duke of Perth's Regiment. He was still with the army at Culloden, whence he managed to escape after the debacle.

After a series of exciting and narrow evasions, he found refuge in Holland and, after a short while, he engaged in the French Army and was posted to Canada where he became A.D.C. to Montcalm. When Quebec fell to the British, he returned to France where, despite the service that he had rendered his adopted country, ungrateful government allowed him to end his life in poverty.

The Chevalier occupied his years of retirement in writing an account of his adventures during 1745 and 1746, of his escapes and of his experiences in Canada. He illustrated his tale with many delightful maps and plans. His entire manuscript still exists and is preserved in the Clan Macpherson's Museum.

Despite small inaccuracies which may be attributed to lapses of memory, the Chevalier's memoirs are of interest that goes far beyond his first-hand account of the last Jacobite Rising. His description of social life in Scotland and in France is excellent. His comments on contemporary conditions are both interesting and valuable, though frequently pungent and prejudiced—but nane the waur o' that!

EVERYDAY LIFE

A BED-SMOOTHER
Seen in the old Weavers' Cottage at Kilbarchan, Renfrewshire.
(National Trust for Scotland.) 4½ miles W. of Paisley, between
A. 761 and A. 737.

BED-MAKING

In small houses with large families, space was valuable. It was found practicable to give the living-rooms a double purpose by building box-beds into them, which could be screened off during the day.

The box-beds are seldom seen, nowadays. They looked like deep presses *(anglicé* cupboards) set back and filling an entire wall, from floor to ceiling. Within them, sometimes as double-deckers, were set the beds and a curtain was drawn across them to separate and to hide them from the rest of the room.

The width of double-beds and, too, their being set back against the wall, there was a certain amount of difficulty involved in making them after their occupants had risen in the morning. Some of the trouble was saved by employing a long, strong blade, made of oak, of rosewood or of deal, with a handle at one end. After the housewife had knelt on the bed in order to tuck in the bedclothes on the wall side this instrument was used to smooth the sheets and blankets in the last stages of bedmaking before the curtains were drawn across and the room prepared for the day.

A few bed-smoothers may still be seen. No longer being of service, though, most of them have disappeared—probably used as firewood.

CANDLE-SNUFFERS *(Sheffield Place)*
(Author's Collection)

CANDLES AND SNUFFERS

There is no system of artificial lighting which can make a better display on a formal dinner table than do candles, set in fine candlesticks or candelabra of silver or of Sheffield plate, throwing a warm glow over everything.

Church candles are made of the same material as were those of the earliest days, still remaining the best substance for the purpose—pure bees-wax. Household candles may possibly be made of bees-wax but, more frequently, they are manufactured from a composite mixture of paraffin-wax and bees-wax or, indeed, of paraffin-wax alone. Candles made of pure tallow were used until well into the present century. They were cheap—and they smelled abominably. Still within living memory, country housewives used to make rushlights by dipping peeled rushes repeatedly into melted tallow until they were thick enough to use for lighting the room.

In all old-fashioned candles, the wick was made of cotton which, burning away slower than the wax, gradually extended farther and farther, bending over and guttering unpleasantly as the wax melted away from around them. Candle-snuffers were introduced to remedy this.

Snuffers, frequently made of silver, acted like scissors to cut off the projecting wick from the top of the candle, and they were fitted with a small receptacle for the clipped and charred piece of cotton, to prevent it from falling onto the table. They stood, too on their own small legs, to keep the dirtied metal from marking the table-linen or the polished table-tops.

Modern invention has developed candlewicks which burn away at the same speed as the wax. Snuffers have therefore passed out of use, being no longer required, so today we find them only as decorative articles in glass-topped tables.

BRASS CREAM-SKIMMERS *(18th-19th Century)*
(Author's Collection)

KITCHEN SKIMMERS

In the days before tinned foods, when families were large and households full, the kitchen was invariably the busiest room in the house. Old prints and pictures show the elaboration of cooking utensils and appliances that were used, even in fairly recent days—spits, grills, copper pans, brass and iron pots. with a multiplicity of other articles whose use can now only be guessed at.

Many such things appear, anonymously and highly priced, in the windows of antique shops. Many more lie unheeded and forgotten in attics. They are worthwhile hunting out, for, with a very little cleaning, they are more than decorative though they are more likely to be hung on the wall than used, nowadays.

Many culinary processes demand skimming. The stock-pot had to be skimmed constantly and so did the home-brewed beers and the country wines. There were few farmhouses where the wife did not keep a wide bowl of milk simmering, from which she would skim the clotted cream— a delightful addition to many dishes, which used to be common enough in Scotland but which seems now to have disappeared everywhere in Britain save for the extreme south-western parts of England, in Devon and Cornwall.

The illustration shows cream skimmers which were last in regular use at the turn of the century.

Link Snuffers in Charlotte Square, Edinburgh.

LINK SNUFFERS

Although Edinburgh's streets were lit by gas quite early in the 1800s, it remained advisable for people to provide their own, additional illumination in order to make their way home safely, in the New Town, whether travelling by sedan chair or on foot. Torches known as links, were the usual lights that were used and link-boys waited outside the music halls and assembly rooms, offering their services.

At the end of the journey, the link-boy used to extinguish his torch, for the sake of economy, and special snuffers for this purpose were included in the wrought-iron railings and domestic lamp-standards in front of many private houses.

Some of these snuffers still survive and they serve a decorative purpose even though their practical use is a matter of historical memory only. Charlotte Square, in Edinburgh, has a fine display to recall the days of not so long ago, when the municipal amenities which, today, we take for granted, were far less efective—even if they existed at all.

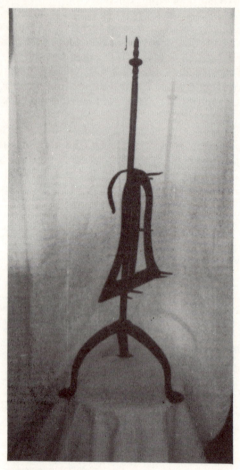

TOASTER *(16th-17th Century)*
(Author's Collection)

AS GOOD AS NEW

Most of us are possessed in some measure of what the Elephant's Child called "satiable curtiosity". Wandering around old junk-yards, peering into attics and stores, odds and ends of old tools and implements are always turning up. Quite obviously they were designed for some specific use and, equally obviously, they have been superseded by something more modern, have been discarded or thrown out and their original purpose has been forgotten.

Some while ago, I discovered an oddly shaped article, lying in the back of a smithy. The smith had no use for it and sold it gladly for a few coppers. I brought it home with me and I still have it.

It consists of an upright rod, which stands on three legs. A frame is held to the rod by rings, so that it is free to run up and down. A spring holds it in position and it has three double-prongs and two single ones sticking out at the front. At the back is a handle for moving the frame up and down, to put it where it happens to be required.

I was completely at a loss to know what the thing was, and nobody seemed to be able to tell me. However, I found that it was extremely useful at tea-time. Pieces of bread were held securely by the double prongs and, placed in front of an open fire, they were toasted without my having to stoop down while using an ordinary toasting-fork. It did splendid service until 'smokeless zoning' made it illegal to use open fireplaces.

It was then that I took its photograph, which I sent to the curator of a museum devoted to the oddities of fairly recent antiquity, asking him whether he had any information about its original purpose.

He had. It was delightful, though not altogether surprising to learn that my 'toasting-tool' is fairly old, though I was not prepared to learn that it is possibly as old as the seventeenth or even the sixteenth century.

As for its purpose—it had been made for exactly the work that it had been doing for me. In fact and indeed, it was designed to be a toaster! It remains as serviceable and as useful today as it was when the smith first made it, three or four hundred years ago.

NUT ROASTERS
(Author's Collection)

NUTS IN—AUTUMN

We are told that the old rhyme about gathering nuts in May is probably a corrupted version of a romantic song which told of lovers gathering knots of may-flowers. This seems to be a very probable explanation of words which appear to be a nonsense. The time for gathering nuts is, of course, not the Spring but the Autumn!

Even today, nut-roasting plays a mystical part in Hallowe'en celebrations. Pairs of nuts are put on the hob, to jump together or else to separate according to the fortunes of the boy and girl for whom they were named and who use this way of divining their fate during the coming twelvemonth. The hob, however useful for fortune-telling, supplies little space for roasting nuts for a large family. For that purpose, special utensils had to be made.

Nut-roasters are still to be seen occasionally, though many people fail to recognise them or have forgotten their use. Some folk, seeing them, imagine that they are warming-pans, used to air beds. This is a silly mistake, because it should be obvious that they would neither hold water nor carry glowing charcoal in any sort of safety!

The nut-roasters illustrated are two which were used until quite recent days. That on the right has been owned by the writer's family for over a century-and-a-half and it was still in use after the First War. The one on the left was rescued from being disposed of for "salvage" when one of Edinburgh's last vendors of hot roasted nuts gave up business. There are many who will still remember him and his companions, standing beside their portable charcoal grates, selling hot nuts at the Mound and beside the Register House. Very welcome they were, coming home late on a cold winter's night!

What is noteworthy, in these days of stark utilitarianism, is the delightful decoration and the artistry of design which went into the manufacture of articles of everyday use. But this seems always to be the case when objects have been made by the skilled hand of a craftsman who took pride in his work and who took pride, too, in making each thing that he made just a little bit different from the others.

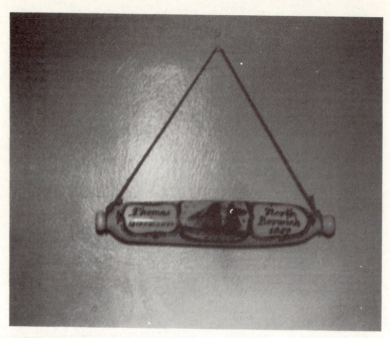

A SAILOR'S LOVE-TOKEN
In the Museum of Huntly House, the Canongate, Edinburgh.

LABOURS OF LOVE

Love-tokens, given by young men to their sweethearts, have long formed an important and interesting part of Scotland's folk-art. They take many forms.

Not so long ago, in our grandparents' or great-grandparents' days, a country lad would show his affection by giving his lass some pirns (bobbins) for lace-making, which he had cut from wood or from bone and had decorated with whorls, dots and spirals. An interesting custom, attached to these pirns, was that they had to be weighted at their bottom end and that one of the beads, threaded to make the weight, must always be blue. Blue being traditionally a safeguard against misfortune or ill-wishing by someone who was *droch-shuileach* or possessed of the evil eye.

Another love-token, which would not be given until the courtship had ripened into an engagement—or 'an understanding' at the very least—

was a collection of bone stay-busks, even more elaborately carved and decorated than the pirns.

Sailors had manners that were different from those of the landsfolk. Their love-tokens were often different, too, and it is strange to find that one of their favourite gifts was was just that thing which formed the music-hall emblem of a hen-pecked husband—a rolling pin! The gift would not be an ordinary, wooden rolling-pin, of course. It would be specially bought, made of glass or porcelain, and long hours at sea would be spent in decorating it before it was considered worthy of being presented. They almost always bore the name of the giver and the port whence he came. Sometimes they had the girl's name painted on them, too—but this is found less frequently and may well be due to the sailor's fear lest the girl should have changed her mind during his absence at sea. If no particular name were written, the gift could still be used to give to someone other than the faithless one!

However, a good few rolling-pin love-tokens bore the girl's name painted on them, some were decorated with pictures of flowers, and still more bore pictures of the sailor's ship. The pictures may have been somewhat stylised and inaccurate, whilst the gaudiness of their colours would hardly qualify them for exhibition in an art gallery. Still, it was the thought that mattered and we may be certain that many a fisher-lass would have preferred one of her lad' gifts to a dozen paintings by Academicians.

The rolling-pin in the photograph is now amongst the collections in Huntly House, in Edinburgh's Canongate. John Jackson of North Berwick painted it with a picture of the schooner *Phoenix* and gave it to an un-named lass in 1857. It was a North Berwick fisherman who told me, many years ago, that these rolling-pins were never intended for ordinary use. They were hung on the wall as soon as they had been received and were only taken down to be used in preparing pastry for a wedding tea. Pastry rolled by one of these pins was reckoned to bring good luck, fair winds and fine catches to everyone who tasted it.

Although glass rolling-pins were made in several places in England, the opaque, creamy-white glass of this one is an indication that it was made in Alloa, in Fife, where alone such glass was produced.

WORLD WAR I: IMMUNITY BADGE
Writer's Collection,

BADGE OF IMMUNITY

In all wars, the fighting man has tended to look askance at the civilian worker, even though it was the latter who provided the sinews of war. This feeling continued into World War II, even though universal conscription had ironed out most of the anomalies and weeded out the majority of the skrimshankers. During the Great War of 1914-1918 feelings ran extremely high, as men returning to the trenches compared their lot and miserable pay with the conditions under which those at home kept regular hours and, too, drew pay for overtime.

It was not only the men in the Forces who felt a grudge against the civilians at home. Girls, too, and women of an age to know better, jeered at men out of uniform and, for a while, indulged in the habit of 'decorating' them with white feathers in the streets of the big towns.

It was found necessary to provide some sort of protection for men who were engaged in essential war work, and badges were issued to them, to be worn in the lapel as a distinguishing sign. Latterly these were made and issued by the Government. To begin with, though, it was left to individual firms to supply their own.

Occasionally these badges still turn up. The one illustrated is in the writer's collection and was provided by one of Edinburgh's oldest engineering firms. It served to mark its employees as being engaged in work of national importance.

BRASS TINDER BOX
(Author's Collection)

FLINT AND STEEL

Before lucifer matches were invented, the striking of flint and steel was almost the only way of lighting a fire. The spark that they produced was not particularly hot, of course, and it needed to be "nursed" in order to obtain a flame.

The spark was struck on to something that would catch fire easily—tinder—consisting of such things as charred linen, cobwebs and so on. This tinder was kept in boxes, usually made of brass, with a hinged lid and with a loop at the back so that they could be hung on the wall, conveniently to hand.

Tinder boxes, both plain and ornamented, are not uncommon in Scotland today. They have lost their original purpose, though, and usually serve as convenient receptacles for bits of string and other domestic odds and ends.

TRADES & INDUSTRIES

THE GILLESPIE BROTHERS' SNUFF MILL
Huntly House Museum, the Canongate, Edinburgh.

SNUFF AMONGST THE SCOTS

Snuff-taking, the hallmark of the Age of Elegance, remains a not uncommon habit in Scotland and at least one big Glasgow Tobacco firm still devotes much time to its production. Fine snuff-mulls, usually made of ram's heads, magnificently decorated with silver, circulate in the Messes of most Scottish Regiments and, too, in many dining-rooms of the old Freemasons' Lodges, to say nothing of Burgh Council-rooms and the stately clubs of the cities. Snuff-taking remains common, too, amongst printers and compositors who, at one time, were forbidden to smoke at work.

Amongst the foremost manufacturers of snuff were the brothers Gillespie who, in the latter years of the 18th century, owned a flourishing tobacconist's business eastward of the Mercat Cross in Edinburgh's High Street. Their business flourished to such an extent that the brothers felt themselves sufficiently wealthy to adopt the habits of the nobility and, accordingly, they bought themselves a splendid coach and decorated its panels with an armorial design. Seeing them driving through the streets in such splendour prompted the Hon. Henry Erskine to produce the famous epigram,

>Wha wad hae thocht it,
>That nebs should hae bocht it!

The brothers' fortune did not disappear in wordly display, however. When James Gillespie died, in 1797, he left his whole estate together with £9,300 for the "founding and endowing of a hospital and charitable institution within the City of Edinburgh or suburbs, for the ailment and maintenance of old men and women".

The foundation was altered in 1870, when its terms were changed to provide the means of building and endowing Gillespie's High School for Girls which remains one of Edinburgh's most notable places of education to this day.

TOBACCONIST'S SIGN
Brechin, Angus

TRADESMENS' SIGNS

Scotland has a sad dearth of the brightly coloured signs which hang outside English inns—we seem to be content with writing the name and leaving it at that. We have other signs, though, which strike the visitor's eye as soon as he comes into Scotland on his journey northwards. Ours are not pub signs but trade signs.

Great, golden pestles-and-mortars stand over the doors of chemists' shops. Tall riding-boots mark the entrance to shoe-shops and to saddlers' too. Golden fish and ox mark fishmongers and fleshers (which, in Scotland, are not identical with butchers) . . . one could compile a very long list.

Tobacconists, whose businesses have been long-established, frequently display signs which differ in several ways from those shown by other trades. They show a human figure and these are not painted gold but are brightly and naturally coloured.

The tobacconists' signs always show a Highlander in the act of taking a pinch of snuff. Sometimes he is dressed in the scarlet coat and regimental kilt of Napoleonic times. At other times he may be wearing a drover's garb. His pose and his dress seem to be different wherever he is met, the two essential things, though, are that he must always be a Highlander and he must be taking snuff.

He is a colourful figure and is more commonly encountered than many people believe. You will meet him in most cities, if you keep your eyes open for him, an attractive, colourful and interesting little figure who is peculiarly Scottish.

BAITING-UP THE LANG-LINE
Photograph taken at Dunbar, at the turn of the century.
(Author's collection)

FISHING WITH THE LONG LINE

Fishing with the "lang-line" is traditional along the East Coast, where the men go out to the fishing and the women's task is to prepare and bait the lines. It was trifle saddening, some years ago, to see the old craft disappear when creel-fishing for partans and lobsters became more profitable. Time reverses most things, however, and the lang-line is back in use again as crabs and lobsters have become rarer along the East Lothian and Berwickshire coasts.

The usual bait is mussels, which are brought up from Holy Island and from as far away as Boston, down on the Wash. The reason is, of course, that Edinburgh has caused the Forth to become so polluted with discharges of untreated sewage that the mussels in the firth are no longer fit to be used and even Musselburgh has lost the reason for its name.

Today's lassies are learning from their grandmothers how to get the lines ready. First the mussels must be taken from their shells, and this may well be an indoor job. Constant practice brings considerable skill and I have been told that a speed of more than a thousand shelled mussels in a single hour is not unusual.

After the mussels have been shelled, the line must be baited. The bait is carefully placed on the hooks, which are tied to snoods—short pieces of line which hang from the main, long line.

As each hook is baited, the line is coiled down into the long wicker basket, known as a scull. This is a task which calls for a remarkable degree of skill, for the line must be so laid down as not to catch or snarl when it is run out. Each baited hook is laid carefully to the side, the line is coiled down and the coils are separated by sheets of newspaper.

With the scull filled, the women's work is finished. It is the man who carries it down to the yawl and stows it away. This, I feel, is connected with the taboo on women approaching the boats when they were being prepared for fishing. When I was a lad, I frequently saw fishermen turn back to their home, prepared to wait until the next tide, if they happened to meet a woman on their way down to the harbour. Perhaps they still do this—the men who fish from small boats along the East Coast have their own beliefs and their own peculiar customs to which they hold fast.

The photograph was taken in Dunbar, some seventy-five years ago. Save for the costume, it would serve for one of today's lassies baiting-up at St Abbs or at any of the other fishing villages where, once again, the long line goes to sea.

THE BASKET HILT OF A BROADSWORD
(Carried in the Forty-five and now in the Clan Museum of the Macphersons, Newtonmore)

120

THE HIGHLAND BROADSWORD

The broadsword is frequently mis-named as 'claymore'. It is, in fact, a very different weapon. Its only connection with the claymore is that from which it derives its own name. This came about through claymore-blades having been cut down in length and employed to make the blades of the new, smaller and handier weapon. They still kept their original, great breadth, however, and thus came to designate the broadsword.

The broadswords most commonly seen in museums and collections are those which were made in the 17th and 18th centuries. Their blades were, for the most part, imported from Europe and many of them bear the inscription of "Andrea Ferrara"—although it is doubtful whether any of them were actually made by that craftsman.

The ornamental basket-hilt of the broadswords are of many designs and all of them are fine pieces of craftsmanship. Notable amongst their makers were the Glasgow Gild of Hammermen, who were the King's Armourers from 1683 until the last of the Loyalist Risings in 1745. In the early decades of the 18th century, the Allan family, in Doune and Stirling, were famous forgers of basket hilts.

The hilts which were made by Glasgow's craftsmen were used by both armies during the Forty-five. Many of them were included in the levy which Prince Charles requisitioned from the city. Glasgow, however, was largely of Hanoverian sympathy and, immediately after the Jacobite army had marched southwards, raised a regiment of six hundred men. The Glasgow Regiment fought in the Battle of Falkirk, in January 1746, when the Hanoverian forces were soundly beaten by those of the Prince in the last-but-one of the major engagements during the Rising.

The blades used in the broadswords are of magnificent temper and many of the weapons, surviving from as long as three centuries ago, are as good today as ever they were. They provided a comfortable grip within the strong protection of the basket hilt and their heavy pommels gave the broadswords a splendid balance, so that they were easily swung and equally effective in the lunge as they were in the cut. Their design made them unsurpassed, even today, in perfection as weapons for hand-to-hand fighting.

The broadsword was essentially a practical weapon, designed and used for fighting. The beauty of its design, though, gives it a place where, amongst all the complicated utilitarianism of modern weaponry, it survives still to give flourish and panache to Scottish military dress.

AN CLAIDH MOR
The Claymore, or Great Sword

AN CLAIDH MOR (THE CLAYMORE)

The basket-hilted sword that is still worn by officers of the Highland regiments is not in fact a 'claymore' although it is frequently misnamed as such.

The *claidh mòr* (*anglice*: claymore) was a huge weapon, with a blade which in some instances was six-feet and more in length. The fact that it was used in battle makes this sword unique in military history, for the only swords of comparable size are those which used to belong to princes of the German States, and those were not for fighting but were the instrument of the executioner's trade.

Too long to be carried at the hip, either in a frog or slung from a baldrick, the claymore was carried vertically, down the spine of its bearer. Its hilt projected over the head and the sword could only be drawn by pulling it upwards and forward.

Its weight made it impossible for the claymore to be used like other swords. It could not be lifted and brought down in a cut, like a sabre, nor could it be darted forward in a lunge. Instead, it was swung sideways, using both hands, in a wide-sweeping, "mowing" swing.

The claymore remained the peculiar weapon of the Highlanders and Islesmen from quite early days through until the 16th century, and some may have been employed in battle at even later dates. That in the illustration is at Moy Hall, is owned by Mackintosh of Mackintosh and is known to have been wielded during the Battle of the North Inch of Perth when Clans Chattan and Kay met, by royal command, in the presence of Robert III and his court, to settle, by force of arms, the vexed question of tribal supremacy in the Central Highlands.

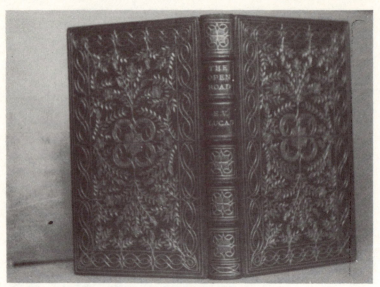

Book bound in Green Morocco, inset with Red Morocco and tooled in Gold.

Modern Reproduction of 18th Century Scottish Bookbinding.

BOOKBINDING

From the first invention of writing, the only way of reproducing a book was by the slow and careful process of manuscript copying. Even after a printing process had been developed, the making of type and the pressing operations remained so slow that every book was an article of value. The sheets which comprised a volume had, therefore, to be protected and it was thus that the craft of the bookbinder came into being. This craft was carried on quite independently of the actual book-reproduction processes and was a highly developed and very individual business.

The traditional material for covering books was wood. The thin wooden boards which formed the covers were themselves covered with leather and this latter was ornamented by tooling, by gold decoration, or even by the insertion of jewels. The result was that, on occasion, the bindings were even more valuable than the book which they were designed to protect.

The actual processes involved in the bookbinders's craft are almost unchanged today from what they were a thousand years ago. Both tools and materials remain as they have always been. The only real innovation has been the substitution of card for wooden boards in making the covers. Even here we find an echo of old times, because the name Card-*board* derives from its original purpose, which was to act as a substitute for wood board in bookbinding.

Scottish bookbinders were noted throughout Christendom at a very early date and many examples of the elaborate and beautiful work of old Scots monastic craftsmen still survive. In spite of mechanisation, craftsmen still continue their traditional work in this country. The illustrations show something of this. The first is a leather-bound and gold-tooled book, the work of a disabled ex-officer in Scotland, which recently won a major fine arts award. The second photograph shows how the work of old Scots craftsmen still sets a standard for modern designers. It shows a modern machine-bound book which reproduces on its covers the tooled design of an 18th century Scottish bookbinder.

CRAFTSMAN'S HUMOUR
18th Century Door-knocker.
(Author's Collection)

THE ARTIST-CRAFTSMAN

There were no demarcation troubles amongst the craftsmen of former days. If they commenced a job, they were prepared to carry it though all its stages. The world is the richer for the way in which they expressed their ideas and notions.

Given a free hand, the ancient craftsmen, who were also artists in many cases, set about their work happily and frequently showed a sense of humour that is sadly lacking from modern, machine-made objects. There was a charmingly affectionate irreverence, too, about the manner in which they applied much of their work to sacred buildings. In Melrose, for instance, a pig is seen playing the bagpipes. Many medieval pew-ends were oddly decorated. Still more frequently humourous scenes appear on the small ledges, called misericords, which were fastened underneath the tip-up seats in the cathedral choirs and which allowed the monks to take some of their weight off their weary feet during the singing of the long, long Offices of the Church. Cheating ale-wives receiving their just punishment, scolding women being chastised by outraged husbands and disobedient schoolboys being soundly tawsed or caned—these are only a few of the thousands of comical carvings, showing scenes from everyday life, which were so frequent in the old buildings.

We can see, therefore, the humour expressed by artist-craftsmen has a very long tradition behind it. It continued until the individual was put out of business by the development of cheap methods of mass-production. Perhaps even this would not have killed off the old skills if it has not been for the change in popular taste which has insisted that design shall be both utilitarian and humourless and, above all else, completely lacking in originality. Perhaps the modern vogue for "gonks" shows the first stirring of a revolt. One could hope so!

Old traditions die hard. The door-knocker in the photograph was made about two hundred years ago—long after the medieval craftsmen had died, but when their ideas still survived. Today, it stands guard on a door in the Highlands, looking after a representative of the family that has owned it ever since it was made. There must be many people who still remember the charming old grotesque when he was, for several decades, a kenspeckle figure on the door of a house in Manor Place, in Edinburgh's West End.

APOTHECARIES' GLASSES, (*Leith Monopoly*)
Writer's Collection

SCOTTISH GLASS

The first glass-works recorded in Scotland were those at Wemyss, in Fife, where Sir George Hay was granted a patent for glass-making in 1610.

Some ten years later the works were still producing "braid glass" for windows, and the Privy Council appointed a commission to inspect and to try the products. They reported favourably, saying that it was as good as 'Danskine' glass, though they could have wished to find it "thicker and tewcher". They thought less of the quality of the drinking glasses, though, and recommended that patterns of English glass be brought to Edinburgh, to be used as a standard of comparison. On the strength of this report, Sir George Hay was granted a Scottish monopoly against foreign glassmakers upon certain conditions, one of which was that the price of 'braid glass' should not exceed 'twalf punds the cradle'.

Fife did not long held its monopoly. In 1689, Leith too was making green bottles and also 'chemistry and apothecary glasses', and it is recorded that its produce was 'in greater quantity in four months than was ever vended in the kingdom in a year, and at as low rates as any corresponding articles from London or Newcastle'. Accordingly the Privy Council made an order which prohibited the import of foreign bottles—and the term 'foreign' included English products, of course. At the same time, Leith was given the privileges of a manufactury, on condition that no greater charge than half-a-crown should be charged for each dozen bottles.

The illustration shows Apothecaries' Glasses, inscribed with their capacity, of green glass, made in Leith.

JOURNEYMAN'S "SAMPLE" TABLE
(Author's Collection)

JOURNEYMEN-CRAFTSMEN

In the days before mass-production in factories, the travelling crafts-man was a kenspeckle figure of Scottish life in the countryside and, no less, in the towns. He brought with him a number of small models which showed in miniature the sort of work that he was prepared to make to order. Having completed his round, he would return to his workshop to make whatever his customers required and these he would deliver when next he passed on his journeying, six months or even a year later.

Many journeymens' models have survived and they tend to escape notice because their smallness causes people to think that they are nothing more than dolls-house furniture. But even a cursory examination will immediately disperse any notion of their being mere playthings. Their workmanship is exquisite.

The little table illustrated is less than six inches high. Its twelve legs are beautifully turned, tenoned and morticed. Its tiny drawers slide in and out; the table flaps fold down on minute, hand-made hinges. It is a wonderful example of a craftsman's work—even though a prospective customer would almost certainly ask for the design to be modified when it came to making the full-sized table. With so many legs, it would other-wise be a most uncomfortable article of dining-room furniture, for it would be almost impossible to sit at it without finding oneself up against a leg!

The modern successors of the old journeymen travel now in cars and all that they carry is a small suitcase filled with tins and with plastic-handled brushes and, possibly, a catalogue too. They make nothing, but only distribute stuff that has been made in bulk by a firm whose very name, in all probability, means nothing, for it has long since been swallowed up in some vast combine. Today's traveller is a poor substi-tute for the craftsman who preceded him.

A MILLER'S PICK
At Prestonmill, East Lothian: National Trust for Scotland.
(Beside B.1407)
(O.S. Sheet 63: 595779)

132

TOOL OF A VANISHING TRADE

When a tool passes out of common use, it gets laid aside and its purpose is forgotten. Barns, smithies, lofts and attics, all over Scotland, hold bits and pieces of articles which were once in everyday use but which were put away when something more modern had made them old-fashioned. The old, discarded tools are now, too often, regarded as mere rubbish, fit only to be thrown away.

The tool in the illustration looks remarkably like a modern geologist's hammer. As a matter of fact, its use was much the same, for it, too, was used for cutting into stone. When the National Trust for Scotland was restoring the old mill near Preston, in East Lothian, this tool was discovered lying about and was immediately recognised as being a miller's pick. It was used for cutting into the grooves in the millstones. deepening them when they became worn down in grinding.

We seldom are able to obtain stone-ground meal in these days—and the loss is ours. The old ways of milling have mostly passed. There still remain a few craftsmen, however, who not only know the tools of their craft but are also able to employ them. One such is the miller who, today, at an age when most men would have retired, is custodian at Prestonmill. He shows the ancient machinery with pride and needs very little persuasion to demonstrate the use of the old tools—including this pick.

ROADS, BRIDGES AND FERRIES

THE WELL OF THE LECHT
Five miles from Tomintoul (A.939)
(O.S. Sheet 38: 151235)

COCKBRIDGE TO TOMINTOUL

General Wade receives credit for recognising that the events of the Jacobite Rising in 1715 had demonstrated the necessity for military roads through the Highlands. His name is now so firmly attached to the road-making projects through the glens and across the passes that, today, most of the 18th century roads are referred to as "Wade's Roads". Wade's work, started in 1725, ended before 1740. A far greater mileage was built by his successors.

General Clayton and General Sir John Cope (the Johnnie Cope of the satirical Jacobite ballad) both extended the system of roadways through the Highlands and, although their work was interrupted by the Forty-five, it was resumed almost immediately upon the cessation of hostilities and was continued until as late as 1790, still under military supervision and, to a great extent, by military labour.

In 1749, General George Churchill was Commander-in-Chief of the troops in "North Britain" and, under his overall command, men of the Welsh Fusiliers built the highway from Blairgowrie to Spital of Glenshee. The road was continued to Braemar, along the line of what is now the A.93, by detachments of Guise's Regiment (the Royal Warwicks). It was not until 1753 that a further extension, north-westwards through the mountains, was commenced by four companies of the 33rd Foot (The Duke of Wellington's), who took the work forward by stages, first to Corgarff, thence to Tomintoul and finally to Grantown-on-Spey, thus making the modern A.939 main road.

The conditions under which the soldiers worked must have been appalling, for the road between Tomintoul and Cockbridge is invariably the first to be blocked by snow at the beginning of winter and, similarly, is always the last main road in Scotland to be freed from snow in the spring. The men's accommodation was, for the most part, makeshift and of a temporary nature. Their rations reached them at irregular intervals and there were times when, during the long winters, they suffered acutely from hunger which, on occasion, brought them to the verge of starvation.

Two memorials remain to remind us of the men who built the road. The name Cockbridge—a single English name amongst all the Gaelic placenames—recalls the building which served as a canteen, which the homesick Englishmen called The Cock Inn. The other reminder is a whitewashed stone, with the letters drawn in with black paint, which the soldiers erected and which the County Council maintains as their memorial.

Travellers along the road that links Deeside and Strathspey could do far worse than halt beside the Well of the Lecht, five miles southward from Tomintoul, and spare a grateful thought in memory of the exiled soldiers from the Midlands of England whose labour made their present journey possible.

WADE'S STONE, *A.9 Perthshire*
(O.S. Sheet 48: 692792)

WADE'S STONE

Although the Great North Road (A.9) follows the route of General Wade's road through the Central Highlands, every now and then it diverges from the old military road whose line still shows green on the hillsides.

A short distance south of Dalnaspidal, an A.A. telephone box by the roadside stands opposite a short section of the original road, showing where the present highway has cut across what used to be a corner. The by-passed loop is clear to the eye, not only because the shape of the old road is distinct but because, since recent years have brought tourists to the Highlands in large numbers, the spot has been a favourite over-night stopping-place for holiday makers, who appear to have small compunction about leaving clear signs of where their caravans have rested—tins, broken bottles and wastepaper (as well as more unsavoury objects) show clearly where the yahoos have broken their journey.

Despite the mess, it is worth-while walking a few yards along the old roadway to look at a tall monolith, a standing stone which towers above it. It marks the spot where General Wade's roadmaking troops, working down from the north, met their comrades who had built the roadway from the opposite direction. This happened in 1729 and the date used to be clearly seen until recent years. Now it is almost completely obliterated by the initials of travellers.

Perhaps this disfigurement of the stone is being done deliberately as tourists endeavour to 'get their own back'. You see, most of the caravans halting by the stone come from England—and, as well as marking the meeting-place of his troops, the stone marks the place where General Wade gave a resounding snub to a party of his English officers.

General Wade was an Irishman and, perhaps on that account, had some sort of fellow-feeling for the Gaels amonst whom he was working and through whose lands he was driving his roads. He was certainly disgusted at the manner in which his English officers liked to mock and jeer at the bare-legged, kilted Highlanders.

One day, he called a party of those officers around him and, standing beside the stone, he instructed them to watch him carefully. Reaching down into the pocket of his breeches, he pulled out a golden guinea, showed it to everyone nearby and then reached up to place it on the top of the stone.

Exactly a year later, Wade called the same group of officers to him, there at the same place. He stretched up his hand, swept it across the top of the stone—and held his guinea high in the air for all to see. The story goes that he completed his demonstration by telling the English in his broad brogue, "Thrue, they may be bare-airsed, but there's not a wan that isn't honest. Oi cud not have done that in *your* counthry, gintlemin!"

THE "GREAT" NORTH ROAD, *(A.9) a few miles from Inverness.*

THE "GREAT" NORTH ROAD

We who live in the Central Highlands feel justly aggrieved regarding our road system. Indeed, it is no system, because there is only one road leading northwards from Perth to Inverness and, unlike main roads in the South, it has no alternative, minor roads, running in the same direction, to relieve it of some of the traffic.

We are held up by caravans, travelling close together, by sightseers, who travel in the middle of the road at 20 m.p.h., watching the scenery and ignoring the lay-bys that have been built at frequent intervals for just that purpose. Tourists, sports enthusiasts and holiday-makers all combine to make the road impassable for those people who need it for the purposes of their daily life. We need it for emergencies, too. Our nearest hospital lies more than fifty miles away . . .

There is a railway, but its trains are too infrequent to give us any convenience of service. British Rail, moreover, has made its fares so high that commercial concerns prefer to crowd the roadway with enormous lorries, finding it cheaper to transport their goods by road than to take them by rail.

Fifty miles at seven miles-an-hour—the accompanying photograph tells the story. What if the following vehicle had been an ambulance with an urgent case aboard? The story would have been the same for there is nowhere that it could have passed.

I said that we feel bitter—and we feel even more so when we read, as we did a few years ago, that the Government was paying many millions of pounds in order to build a new underground railway for London which, in order to save the poor Londoners from walking a few miles, was going to cost the rest of the country at least seven millions every year to make up its deficit. Now, in February 1973, we have been told of more than 2000-million pounds that are to be spent on London's roads. We have to pay taxes to help pay for these London luxuries, whilst we do without necessities. Why the devil should we?

MILESTONES IN FIFE

MILESTONES IN THE KINGDOM OF FIFE

Strictly speaking, the milestones of Fife are not really stones at all; they are cast iron and splendid pieces of work. The County Councillors of bygone days who erected them deserve our thanks, and their present day successors who continue to maintain them are no less worthy of congratulation.

The cost of these milestones must have been considerable, for they were all of them "one off" castings, requiring a separate, individual mould for each.

Some show the placenames in a flowing script, with the names abbreviated to fit the available space—and, presumably, the traveller who didn't know that "Boar^S" directed him to Boarhills either was not interested (in which case it didn't matter) or else he was going to some other place (in which event he just would not be interested).

No farm nor village seems to have been so insignificant as to be unworthy of mention on many of the Fife milestones, though some patterns show the names of townships in larger letters than are accorded to the farms and estates.

Some give the distances in miles, some go into an elaboration of indicating right and left turnings, off the main road, to reach places that lie in directions other than the direct line of the highway.

Other milestones show a heading which tells the traveller where he is. Underneath, the names on the right hand side show villages in that direction and, on the other side the leftward villages are named. No miles are shown on these stones, however.

There are other patterns, too, and their study would make a fascinating subject for somebody's research. Their number and their variety are, I think, peculiar to the Kingdom—but oddities of this nature are only to be expected in those parts, for the men of Fife have always tended 'fur tae gang their ain gait" and their countryside teems with individualities.

THE OLD ROAD – USUALLY SUBMERGED BELOW LOCH LAGGAN, *A.86.*
(O.S. Sheet 36: 426838)

A REAPPEARING ROAD

General Wade's great road over the Corrieyarrick Pass, from Fort Augustus into Strathspey, was closed by weather during at least four months of every year. In 1804, therefore, a very distinguished group of Highland notables addressed a memorandum to Government. The Duke of Gordon, Cluny Macpherson and Mackintosh of Mackintosh were amongst the 'nobility and gentry' who submitted that the old road was too often impassable and that a new highway was both desirable and essential.

Before a new road could be started, it was necessary that a route be surveyed. This task was entrusted to three great engineers, Telford, Rickman and Hope. These were the men who were responsible for opening up much of the Highlands and whose work has been little augmented today, even after the passage of a century and a half.

A line was decided upon, running to Fort William by way of Loch Laggan-side and Glen Spean. Next, the work was put out to contract, each contractor being required to produce guarantees of his efficiency. Troubles began to mount up, right at the start.

In the first instance, the cost of building the forty-two miles of highway were grossly under-estimated. Then the lowest tender was accepted. But the contractor had not even commenced work before his contract was terminated and cancelled, the reason being that he had been discovered to be "a feeble and nerveless worker without anything to lose". The next contractor, Clark, went bankrupt and sought Debtor's Sanctuary at Holyrood, whither he was followed closely by his guarantor. Thirteen years had passed before the road was completed, by John Davidson, at a total cost of £23,500.

In general, the present day A.86 follows the route which Telford surveyed. The old road has, of course, been given a modern surface and, in one or two places, it has been widened.

Improvements are still being carried out along its length. A major task of re-alignment was made necessary when, some years ago, the Hydro-Electric Board announced its plans for the dam below Loch Laggan, which would effectively raise the level of the water and would bring it above the road.

A new loop was built in the old road, and the abandoned stretch was given over to the loch, which very soon covered it. However, Telford's road is still there, hidden under the waters of the dam, and after dry seasons, such as those of recent summers, it appears once again like a ghost from the past. It is still metalled, banked and ditched—and it is quite unusable.

THE END OF ANE AULD SANG
The Queensferry Ferryboat, Mary Queen of Scots, *in the Shipbreaking Yard at Inverkeithing.*

THE QUEEN'S FERRY

Nobody knows when the first ferries ran across the Forth where, nowadays, the two bridges span the firth. It is certain that the Romans had such a service, because their naval base was at the mouth of the Almond, just a short distance to the eastward, and it is inconceivable that they would not have used the short and easy line of communication across the estuary, between their bases and the huge, advanced positions in the hills of Perthshire.

In 1066, after the English had been defeated by the Normans, Prince Edgar, the legitimate heir to the Saxon throne, fled the country by sea, together with his mother and sisters. He aimed at seeking refuge in Hungary, but his ship was driven northwards and the royal party came ashore on the Scottish coast. The place where they landed has, ever since, been known by the name of the Saxon princess, whom Malcolm later married, and is called Margaret's Hope. The line which they took to cross the Forth became The Queen's Ferry.

Before the Reformation, a regular ferry service was maintained as a work of religious charity and was entrusted to the clerics of Dunfermline. No fixed fares were charged and people were trusted to pay according to their rank, status or means. To 'cheat' in payment was, of course, an act of fraud against Mother Church and was a piece of foolishness which could bring bad luck--if nothing worse. Some form of payment had to be made for the crossing, lest ill befall the non-payer. The belief still holds good and many people, crossing the Forth Bridge by train, throw a penny into the water "for luck".

Local fishermen next operated the ferry, independent of any control, until it was felt that affairs should be properly regulated. So, in 1831, a committee of management was established by law and it appointed Mr James Scott, R.N., as Resident Manager, under strict orders to hold himself in readiness *at all times* to give service to passengers.

Rules were made and provided that a boat, a pinnace and a yawl were to be kept on the south side of the ferry and that at least nine men, to crew the boats, were to be resident in South Queensferry or Newhalls. A scale of fares was laid down, too, ranging from ten shillings for a hearse or mourning coach, 8s.6d. for a barouche or landau, and downwards to 3d. for a child. Puppies and Highland shearers were charged the same rate—one penny!

The first steamboat on the Queensferry service commenced work just over 140 years ago. Latterly the ferry was run by the Glasgow firm of Denny Brothers whose four paddle-steamers, *Queen Margaret, Robert the Bruce, Mary Queen of Scots* and *Sir William Wallace,* were still plying between the Hawes Pier and Fife until 1964, when the Road Bridge was opened.

Today, for the first time in two thousand years, no boats ply in a ferry service across the Forth. One thing, however, remains unchanged. We still have to pay in order to pass over between North and South shores of the firth. One wonders why this imposition was placed upon Scotland when in London, nothing is charged to cross such works as the Chiswick and Hammersmith flyovers—bridge-works which were vastly more expensive than the Forth Road Bridge. Most Scots will answer this question in one way. The bridge tolls were imposed by the Government, the Government is in London and . . . the Devil looks after his own!

TURNPIKE BESIDE THE A.9
(O.S. Sheet 48: 766691)

THE TURNPIKE

If there had been no barrier across the highway, nobody would have stopped to pay his toll, so, to make sure of collecting the money that was required for roadworks, some means had to be devised to close the road. Usually gates stood at the end of each stage, but these came at a later period and were seldom found in the Highlands, where transport difficulties prevented the carrying of heavy iron frameworks.

The earliest form of barrier at the toll stages was a wooden pole which, beside the tollhouse, swung on a pivoted upright and, on the other side of the road, rested in a wooden crotch. On the earlier and narrower roads, the swinging pole was supplied by a pike-shaft—hence the still-used name of 'turnpike' for a main road.

In places where toll-gates were used, very many have survived. Iron gates are far too useful to be thrown away and, where formerly they crossed the highways, it frequently requires very little searching, in a very small radius, to discover the old gate, now closing a gap in a hedge or a wall on some nearby farm.

The turnpikes, being of wood, did not survive for long after they had passed out of use. Probably most of them were taken for firewood. One turnpike remained in use until just a few years ago, still employed in closing the road, though not for toll purposes. At the southern end of Drummochter Pass, before Perthshire marches with the County of Inverness, the turnpike was retained in order to warn drivers that the road ahead was impassable because of deep snow.

History has been repeated in an odd way, because the pikeshaft has been replaced in exactly the same way as it predecessors—by gates. The old turnpike still stands on its post, though, beside the old tollhouse. Broken, now, and looking very much the worse for wear, it is well worth more than a merely casual glance, for it is the last survivor in all Britain of a piece of highway history.

Of course, there are still toll-bars, electronic ones, further south along the same road, where the highway crosses the Forth—forced upon Scotland, in defiance of the Highways Act, by a Westminster which could spare millions of pounds for London's needs but which refused as many thousands for Scotland's requirements. Be we won't go into that . . .

GRANITE TRAMS, *Bells Brae, Edinburgh*

TRAMS

When the English talk of 'trams', they mean the vehicles which, until recently, used to run through the streets on rails. In Scotland the word is used more accurately. The conveyances are known as "the cars", whether drawn by horses or by cable, or propelled by electricity. The actual trams are, in fact, the rails along which the cars run.

'Tram' is an old word in Scots, and originally it meant a long thin spar, such as the shafts of a wagon. Later it included all things of a similar shape—even a man's leg-bones, for someone with extra-thin legs is still laughed at for his "spindle trams". Thus, when a trackway was laid through the glaur, the mud of an unmetalled road, its narrow sections were called 'trams' and, where the wheels of a cart ran, they were termed 'tramways'.

Tramways were made of wood, of stone and of iron. They provided a firm support for the wheels whilst, at the same time, they left a space between them where the horse could grip the ground without slipping. They supplied an obvious need in places where heavy loads had to be transported at frequent intervals, such as at the mines. One notable example of this was at Prestonpans where, across the lines, the Highland army of Prince Charles Edward met and routed the Hanoverian troops of General Cope, in 1745, in what was, in effect, the first railway battle.

Stone tramways can still be seen in the towns, where steep hills made things difficult for the horses. Mostly they have been overlaid with macadam and tar, but some remain as they were, with a smooth, stone causey allowing the cartwheels to run easily, while the granite setts, laid crosswise between the trams, give the horses a better grip on the slope.

TOLL COTTAGE AT KILLIECRANKIE *(A.9)*

ROAD TOLLS

During the first half of the 18th century, after the Act of Union, Scottish roads were deplorable. In fact, they were so bad that in 1720 there was not a single chariot or chaise in all the country north of the Tay and, in the middle of the century, it took a whole day for a four-horse coach to travel the sixteen miles of highway between Haddington and Edinburgh.

It was not until 1749 that anyone ventured to provide stage-coach travelling between Edinburgh and Glasgow—twice weekly, fare 9s.6d., and the journey took twelve hours. Small wonder, then, that few people travelled unless they were obliged to do so, and small wonder that sea-passages were preferred to journeys by road!

In 1751, the Turnpike Act came into effect and an assessment upon landlords and farmers, applied to road improvement, made an almost immediate change in conditions and effected a complete revolution in the life of the country.

Local responsibility for the maintenance of roads was, to a great extent, financed by tolls, which were collected from passengers at stages along the highways. Tickets were sold, each one laboriously written out by hand, to permit passage. This system continued until, in 1879, all tolls were abolished by Act of Parliament and the upkeep of the roads became much as it is today.

Names such as the Bearsden Toll still recall the old stages. More apparent to the traveller, though, are the small toll-cottages which stand beside the main roads and which, in a few cases, still show boards or stones bearing the old scale of charges. Solidly-built and, for the most part, still inhabited, these cottages are quite distinctive. An obvious feature of them all is a pair of windows, looking both ways up and down the highway, which enabled the keeper of the toll-house to keep an eye on traffic approach from either side.

History repeats itself. For visitors to Scotland (and few Scotsmen, too) know that the long stretch of dual-carriageway which runs from Edinburgh northwards, joining the M.90 motorway beyond the Forth Road Bridge, is no part of the A.90. By order of Westminster, all that road and the bridge itself are removed from the national road-network. Public Funds neither built the road and bridge, nor do they maintain them. The cost of both fell upon the ratepayers of Midlothian, Edinburgh and Fife As a result, after more than eighty toll-free years, tolls have been reimposed upon the roads of Scotland and, by the same token, highways have been removed from Government control and made the responsibility of local authorities. Every traveller across the Forth is made sadly aware of this retrogressive state of affairs.

THE KING'S HOUSE AT GARBHA MOR
*On General Wade's road over the Corrieyarrick Pass, from
Badenoch into Lochaber. Shown as "Garvamore."*
(O.S. Sheet 36: 529943)

THE KING'S HOUSES

When, after the failure of the Jacobite Rising in 1715, it became obvious that military roads would be needed through the Highlands, the task was given to General Wade. He was succeeded by General Clayton, in 1740, who handed over the duties of Commander-on-Chief in Scotland to General Sir John Cope, in 1743. All three Generals built and extended the roads, whilst the engineering work was principally supervised by Edward Caulfield, with his headquarters in Inverness.

For the most part, these roads followed the line of the tracks which traversed the hills, taking the routes which centuries of experience had shown to be the easiest ways by which to take the cattle droves from the Highlands southwards to the main centres of population.

The hardy hillsmen used to sleep by the wayside. King George's troops, however, required staging-posts where they could obtain shelter and refreshment at the end of each day's march. So it was that existing buildings were adapted or new buildings were erected, to be known as King's Houses and to serve not only the military but also to act as inns for travellers. Some of these King's Houses have fallen into ruin, some still stand although they are now deserted, still others have been incorporated into more modern buildings and some remain hotels.

One King's House which still stands, almost unchanged, is that which used to be the staging-post between Ruthven-in-Badenoch and Fort Augustus, beside St George's Bridge which General Wade erected at Garbha Mor.

Outside the building, the cobblestones, where the cavalry used to bed-down their horses on heather, are now covered with turf. The interior was almost intact until recent years, and the house was still occupied until shortly before the last war. Now, however, it is sad to see that the commercial firm, which owns the King's House and many miles around it, would appear to have no concern for this venerable relic, where Prince Charles is said to have slept on his march southwards and which has been listed as a building of national interest. A few years ago, the gutting of the interior was started when the two box-beds, which took up most of a downstairs room, were pulled out—fortunately, the West Highland Museum in Fort William has rescued one of them from destruction. Stone slates have fallen from the roof, windows are broken and it cannot be long before storm and weather will have done their destructive worst.

If the precedent, set in other parts of Scotland, is followed, we may expect that, in a few years' time, the owners will plead that the building is beyond repair and will ask for permission to demolish it because it is dangerous. There is no sign yet of this being done—equally, though, there is no sign of any preservation work being done.

DIRECTIONS TO ST BRIDE'S BURIAL-GROUND
Beside the A.86, a few yards northward of the bridge over the
River Calder, near Newtonmore.
(O.S. Sheet 37: 706987)

THE GAELIC NOTICE—A THREEFOLD MEMORIAL

Only a generation ago, Gaelic was the everyday language of Upper Strathspey. Now it has been blotted out, quite deliberately, through the policies which Authority decreed for education in the Highlands. The few in these parts who still remember their mother-tongue will tell you, sadly, of how they used to be taught that Gaelic was the crude language of a barbarous race and, too, will recall how they used to be strapped if they dared ever to speak Gaelic within the hearing of the dominie. On all Speyside, only one public notice remains in the old language. It stands beside the A.86, the Fort William Road, a quarter of a mile from its junction with the A.9 and just outside the village of Newtonmore.

From time out of mind *Cladh Bhrighde,* St Bride's Graveyard on the banks of the Calder, has been the last resting-place of the inhabitants of the district in which Newtonmore now stands. Despite this, in 1875, the tenant of Banchor Farm barricaded the way to the cemetery and, with the approval of the superior, proceeded to build a farm-steading across the roadway itself. Protests were ignored, and the people were driven to seek the protection of the law.

Peter Cattanach, an Edinburgh lawyer who had local connections, assisted in raising an action in the Court of Session, lodging a plea for suspension and interdict. The demands were more than reasonable. The complainants did not ask for the destruction of the new buildings— although they would assuredly have been justified in doing so. All that they asked was that the respondents should allow an approach road, with permanent rights of way, to be made from the highway to the burial-ground.

A fair amount of legal pleading and procedure ensued before, finally and in 1876, the case was brought before the Lords Ordinary and an order was issued to give the people considerably more than they had originally asked. Not only were they to be given their rights of access to Cladh Bhrighde, but the road to it was to be constructed at the expense of the respondent and, instead of the former footpath, it was to be built to a uniform width of 12-feet and was to be maintained with a surface fit for the passage of vehicles. Finally, to ensure that no future encroachment should be made upon local rights, a notice was required. This notice is that which stands still by the roadside, just eastward of the Calder Bridge. *An Rathad Daingnichte le Lach. Gu Cladh Bhrighde.* (The Roadway Established by Law. To St Bride's Graveyard.)

The notice is worthy of study, for it serves a three-fold purpose. It demonstrates how common rights may be enforced against would-be usurpation. It guarantees that no future encroachment shall ever be made. And, lastly, it serves as a memorial to the language which an alien government has all but succeeded in wiping out over most of the country.

SHIPS AND SEA

**COASTAL DEFENCES AGAINST
JOHN PAUL JONES.**
*The Battery at Dunbar Harbour,
East Lothian. (A.1087–loop-road
off the A.1.)*

THE U.S.N. AND ITS RENEGADE SCOT

Geographical necessity has compelled Scotland to be a maritime nation and her sailors have won renown throughout the ages. Names that spring immediately to mind are those of Sir Andrew Barton and Sir Andrew Wood, who won tremendous victories over English fleets which far outnumbered those of Scotland; Alexander Selkirk, who was Robinson Crusoe and whose cottage stands marked with his statue in Largo; Admiral Lord Cochrane who, victim of a confidence trick and maligned by English politicians, left the British service, established two Navies in South America and finally returned to make a new name in the Royal Navy; in our own time, Admirals Sir Rhoderick McGrigor and Cunningham—those to name only a few amongst the many. Few Scottish sailors, though, have won such fame as the man who, in 1799, brought a wave of panic to his native shores. This man was John Paul Jones, hailed in the country of his adoption as "Father of the United States Navy" and described in his homeland as "that desperate buccaneer."

When John Paul Jones appeared in the Firth of Forth, he spread alarm and despondency all along the East Coast—nowhere worse than in the Kingdom of Fife. In Kirkcaldy, the minister of the kirk led his flock down to the seashore to pray for winds that should drive Paul Jones back whence he had come. His prayers met with no success whatsoever! Off Pittenweem, the American squadron sailed boldly into the roads and signalled for a pilot. Andrew Paton, the port's only pilot, believing the ships to be British, came out and was taken aboard the flagship. He was still unaware of the ships' nationality (presumably they were flying no ensign) for he asked the admiral if Pittenweem could be spared a supply of gunpowder and shot, to use if Paul Jones should happen to appear off its shores. In a good Scots tongue, he was told that he could load a small supply of powder into his cutter, but that no shot could be spared. The bags of powder were accordingly lowered into the pilot's boat and taken ashore. Paton, however, stayed aboard and was soon disillusioned as to the nationality of the ships and, no less, as to the identity of the admiral to whom he had addressed himself. He was, of course, the same John Paul Jones whose threat had so alarmed the towns along the coast.

Many Scottish islands and harbours still show the defences that were hurriedly built to withstand possible attack by the ships of the United States. Inchgarvie, on which now stands the centre-pier of the Forth Bridge, had fifteenth century fortifications which had been reinforced to withstand attack by Cromwell in 1650, and which were now strengthened once again against the 'pirate' of 1799.

Citizens of the United States, whilst justified in being proud of John Paul Jones (even though he was a Scot!) can hardly take pride in the reason for his sailing into British waters nor in the ultimate effect of his incursion. The American ships, sailing in the name of Liberty, put to sea in support of Napoleon, the tyrant dictator who gave the precedent to Hitler, at a time when the British Navy was fully engaged in fighting the dictator in the Mediterranean and the Channel. The result of Paul Jones' cruise off the East Coast of Scotland was that many harbours were fortified and the fortifications erected against his possible attack, served to house the batteries which formed an effective deterrent to any French thoughts of invasion.

THE GRAND FLEET IN THE FORTH *probably around the year 1906.* (Photograph in Author's Collection.)

The battleships are, I think, those of the King Edward VII Class which, during the Great War, were nicknamed 'The Wobbly Eight', 'The Behemoths', 'The Uriahites' and 'The Mine-bumpers'—being out of date and classed as expendible, they sailed ahead of later and more important ships to clear the minefields and get rid of floating mines.

THE ROYAL NAVY

Scotland's Royal Navy commanded her coasts and, indeed, the whole of the North Sea for several centuries. As early as the 15th century it unique in possessing warships which were not merely converted merchant vessels. In the 16th century, Scottish naval architects and shipwrights were in demand all over Europe and, in particular, in the Scandinavian and Baltic countries, for their skills were unmatched.

In 1513, the Scottish flagship was the great *Michael,* larger than any ship of her time and equal in size to a battleship of Nelson's time. She was described as a ship *qui ne s'en trouve une telle en crestienté,* the like of which was not to be found in Christendom. Nor was she alone. She led thirteen ships-of-the-line, all three-masted, as well as a large fleet of smaller warships and of auxiliaries, including her own, sixty-oar tender.

Our old allies, the French, appealed for help in 1513 and this great fleet put to sea and sailed north-about, to make rendezvous with the French Navy in the Channel. Then came news of Flodden. The Scottish Navy was sold to the King of France and moored in a French port. There it rotted at anchor for want of mariners who were capable of taking the fleet to sea. The Scottish crews had returned home and no sailors in Europe could manage ships whose design and rig were so far in advance of their time.

A few ships still wore the Saltire Ensign until the Treaty of Union with England, in 1707. The newly-established Royal Navy of the United Kingdom deserted Scottish ports until 1906. Then, with war threatened, Rosyth was established to provide a secure base in the event of hostilities. Invergordon and Scapa Flow followed and provided the principal anchorages of the Grand Fleet throughout both World Wars.

When peace has been declared, Naval Bases in Scotland have either been closed or else put on a "care and maintenance" footing. The Navy has, for the most part, returned to its harbours in England, to Portsmouth, Plymouth and the others. Unemployment is left to reign in the North whilst work is provided in the South, at bases which are useless in time of war. This provides a very real grievance which has often been voiced but which remains unheeded.

After the first World War, the German *Hochseeflotte,* the High Seas Fleet, surrendered in the Forth, providing the greatest congregation of ships that the world has ever seen or will see. The Royal Navy stretched from Rosyth to the Isle of May, and the German fleet sailed into the Firth, parallel to the British ships. To all intents and purposes, the Navy has left these waters.

Occasionally, the Forth sees a few vessels of the NATO countries, engaged in exercises in the North Sea. A few minesweepers move up and down and an infrequent submarine of the Royal Navy puts into Rosyth for minor repair or for refitting. It is a sad retreat from greatness— and an even sadder waste of safe anchorages, fine craftsmen and equally fine facilities.

THE BASS ROCK. *Three miles off North Berwich (A.198) at the entrance to the Firth of Forth.*

THE BASS ROCK

Three miles out to sea from North Berwick, the Bass Rock, 350 feet high, towers up as sentinel over the southern approaches to the Firth of Forth. Its sheer cliffs, gleaming white in the sunlight, might be taken for chalk. In fact, their whiteness is the effect of the plumage of thousands of solan geese and of their droppings. The solan geese, or gannets, are so plentiful on the Bass that the rock provided their Latin name of *sula bassana*. Boats may come alongside the small jetty, if the weather is calm, otherwise they may anchor in about five fathoms off the south-western end of the rock in a very small area. Everywhere else the Bass rises sheer from the bottom of the sea. Unexpectedly, it is pierced with a natural tunnel, nearly 200 yards long. Visitors are discouraged from attempting its passage unless they are accompanied by a boatman who knows the place and knows the tides, too.

St Baldred, a disciple of St Mungo, patron of Glasgow, was sent by his master to make a missionary headquarters on the Bass. From his cell there, which forms part of the structure of a medieval chapel, he performed the miracle of transporting a rock on which many ships had been wrecked nearby. He charmed it into floating over to the East Neuk of Fife, where he ordered it to sink—somewhat thoughtlessly, one feels, for it still lies where the saint sent it and, as the Carr Rock, it remains a danger to shipping and nowadays is marked by a lightship, off Fife Ness.

The castle of the Bass was originally built by Malcolm II, King of all Scotland at the time when England formed part of the Danish Empire under Canute. Much restored, the ancient castle was used as a prison for recalcitrant leaders of extremist sects during the years of religious troubles in the times of the Commonwealth and of Charles II. Thereafter, it was captured by a party of Jacobite officers who held it for King James through three years, during which they were supplied by French men-of-war, until they surrendered with the honours of war in 1694. The fortifications were dismantled a few years later.

For 200 years the Bass remained uninhabited save for a few pasturing sheep and the occasional herdsman who came to cull their numbers. Then, on December 1st, 1901, the Bass assumed its present task when, on a night of blinding storm, the lamp of the lighthouse was lit for the first time.

CRAIL HARBOUR, *Fife. A.917, A.918 and B.940.*
Established before 1498 as a 'havin', rebuilt in the 16th century.
Extended in 1828.

SEA-BORNE TRADE

Scotland was a country whose life depended upon trade and, with her one land frontier, that with England, frequently closed, the only trade-roads open to her were those of the sea. The extent of her mercantile traffic is astonishing. She held the monopoly of the enormous market for salt fish in Russia and the Baltic lands. Her people held rights of dual-nationality in France and her merchants made full use of that advantage. In the Netherlands, at Veere, the Scots possessed extra-territorial rights of a Staple, with privileges extending to the exercise of their own laws and religion and extending even to the power to order the ships of any other nation to leave a berth in harbour which, for reasons of convenience, the Scottish skippers wanted for themselves.

Commerce flowed in both directions. One has only to look at the old houses along the East Coast to see how close relations were with Europe. The pan-tiled houses of the old merchants could be transferred to Flanders and no one would notice any difference. Even more surprising is the fact that the language of the East Coast is almost identical with the Frisian dialect. This used to be noticeable when the Netherlands *Hospitaal-Kerkschip*, an auxiliary schooner named *De Hoop*, used to call in at the Scottish fishing-ports. Her crew would talk happily with the Scots fishermen when they came ashore, whilst men from English ships were at a complete loss.

The marvel is that so extensive a trade was accomplished with so few facilities. Places are referred to as 'havens' and held customs posts where, today, even small yachts think twice about coming in to land. Mostly the harbours consisted of little more than a pier or a breakwater—and this on a bleak and exposed coast. The merchant-skippers must have been as brave as they must have been skilled in their craft.

The fairly modern harbour at Crail, in Fife, offers far more than existed in earlier years. Yet Crail alone used formerly to serve as "mother" to no fewer than seven other "ports", where nothing now serves that purpose; and this until the late 18th century.

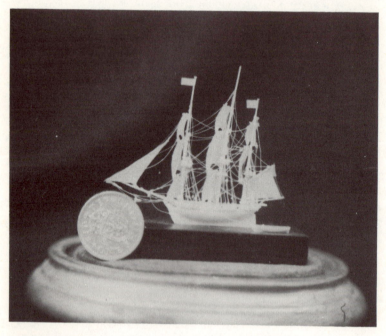

FRENCH PRISONER'S MODEL SHIP, *made in Edinburgh Castle in 1795-6. Its size may be seen by comparison with the shilling, against the wooden base on which the model stands.* (In Author's possession)

FRENCH P.O.Ws.

Everyone who has read R.L.S.'s tale of *St Ives* knows that Revolutionary and Bonapartist prisoners of war were held in Edinburgh Castle. These prisoners whiled away the days of captivity by engaging in various crafts and they earned money by selling the results of their industry to visitors.

Britain's war was conducted at sea for the most part, so it was natural that the majority of the French prisoners were sailors. Many of them, therefore, amused themselves by carving model ships. They used very simple tools, mostly made by themselves, and their materials were just such as came to hand.

Some of the prisoners' models were of considerable size, magnificently made to scale and possessing considerable merit both as examples of craftsmanship and as works of art. They were made either of wood or of bone—the latter probably originating with their rations.

Very small models were made, too, known today as 'bijou' models. Mostly these were made of wood. All those known to have been made in Edinburgh are wooden examples of the craft, save for one only, made of bone. This was the work of a prisoner who had monarchist sympathies and was given by him to my own ancestor, an officer in the French Royal Navy who had escaped at the Revolution and was serving with the British Navy.

The little, bijou model is outstanding in the delicacy of its manufacture. It stands no more than two inches high and yet has every detail carved with wonderful accuracy. Even the lines of the planking are shown and figures of the crew are standing on the deck. The hull, masts and sails are all made of bone. The rigging is human hair.

The measure of its craftsmanship was shown when, a few years ago, I wished to have some slight repairs made to it. The man best qualified to give advice told me to leave well alone. The only man who could make a proper job of it would be a Napoleonic prisoner of war—and they are in rather short supply nowadays!

JUNDIE BITTIES

DUNKELD–*from a position very near to Mr Macgregor's Garden. A.9 (at foot of hill).*

DUNKELD

The tourists' cars stream through Dunkeld, hundreds in every hour, and few stop to look at the town which, more than any other—more even than Edinburgh—displays an epitome of Scotland's history.

In Dunkeld, the Celtic priesthood of Culdees established an Abbey in the year 315—and that was nearly three centuries before St Augustine brought Christianity to the south-eastern tip of England. Here, too, the Scottish Kings made their principal residence in the days when they were still consolidating their realm from its first beginnings in Argyll.

Beside Dunkeld towers Birnham Hill, crowned by King Duncan's Camp, whence the famous, albeit apocryphal march set out for Dunsinane.

Dunkeld Cathedral, dating from the 12th century, stands as a memorial to Scottish piety and, too, to Scottish intolerance. After three hundred years of sanctity, it was desecrated by the Reformers in 1560. In 1689 it was burned by the fanatical Cameronians, formed into a regiment to fight the supporters of King James VII and II. Now partly restored and with many interesting monuments intact, it provides Dunkeld with its parish kirk.

Around the market square, the little houses have been restored by the National Trust for Scotland, so here and in the approach to the Cathedral may be seen how a Scottish market-town appeared in the 17th and 18th centuries.

Across the Tay, in Little Dunkeld, Niel Gow lived and composed the reels and strathspeys which are amongst the finest of all Scottish tunes.

Telford's splendid and beautiful bridge across the river, leading into Dunkeld, tells of how the Parliament of 1800 set a precedent for Westminster to follow in recent years, for the Government then refused to allow money for a bridge on the Great North Road, just as the present day Government refused to build either the Forth Road Bridge or even the roads leading to it. Again building has been enforced upon local authority, in this case upon the Counties of West Lothian and Fife and upon the city of Edinburgh. They were compelled to borrow the money from Westminster and, once again, tolls have been imposed on the Great North Road which, for all their cost, barely suffice to pay the exorbitant interest which Westminster charges on the enforced loan.

It is happier to climb the Hill of Dunkeld, whence the photograph was taken on a site very close to the most famous garden in literature—none other than Mr Macgregor's Garden, where the wonderful Beatrix Potter "saw" the Adventures of Peter Rabbit and wrote her illustrated letters, telling her young friends about it all.

And *still* the tourists stream past, most of them bored with their long journey and wondering why there is nothing interesting to see along the road . . . !

THE JOUGS

THE JOUGS

The people of Scotland don't attend the Kirk as regularly as they used to do and, because of that, morals have declined. So 'they' say, in complete *non sequitur*. Attendance at the services and the preachings have never, in all the country's history, had any real effect upon our native manner of living—no matter how deplorable that may seem to the unco guid whom Burns castigated so bitterly and so brilliantly. The Scots have always been robust in their habits and no less so in their amusements, whilst nothing that the priests of the Auld Kirk nor the ministers of the New Ane could say or do has ever changed the ways of the people.

The Roman Church imposed penances and ecclesiastical punishments that were immeasurably stronger, but all to no effect. The Kirk of the Reformers established what amounted to absolute rule, complete with informers, spies and all the concomitants of totalitarian government to keep things going—and still houghmagandie and fisticuffs (sometimes more than that) remained the popular amusements.

The penalties inflicted by the Kirk were grimly severe. Guilty parties, condemned for offences which seem trivial in the extreme, were ordered to pay heavy fines in increasing sums of money. Offenders were exposed publicly in the churches within all the bounds of a presbytery, to make "circular satisfaction". They were compelled to stand in sackcloth on a bench or a stool in front of the pulpit, there to be admonished by the minister before all the congregation—and this for as many as twenty-six Sabbaths in succession. Even this did not end the punishment, for even when their weeks of suffering in the church were completed they were liable to spend a further number of Sabbaths chained to the kirkyard wall, still dressed in sackcloth.

Continuing evidence of the kirk's interpretation of Christian mercy is still to be seen hanging from many walls, outside the old kirks where the jougs, which secured the victims by the neck whilst they 'tholed their dule', are met so frequently that it would be a waste of time to list them.

Those illustrated hang beside the kirkyard gate at Duddingston, beside the Queen's Park in Edinburgh.

Lepers' Squinch in Dunkeld Cathedral, Perthshire. A.9.
(O.S. Sheet 56)

LEPERS

The Jewish Law declares that lepers are "unclean", and it is this notion of uncleanness, surviving even today, which lies behind the horror with which leprosy is still regarded. In medieval times, lepers were completely outcast in many countries and were subjected to strict regulations to make sure that they did not come into contact with other people. Nowadays we have changed all that—we hide lepers away in isolation hospitals where they are forgotten. In the Middle Ages they were at least allowed to emerge from behind walls and barriers.

Modern medical science has decided that many who, in old days, were included amongst the lepers, did not suffer from leprosy but from a dietary deficiency which gave a leper-like appearance to the skin. In Scotland, and in England too, there must have been many such. In the Northern Kingdom, however, the lepers were far less heavily penalised than they were in the south—or, indeed, than they were in any other country in Europe. This kindness may have been due in part to a national spirit of tolerance. It certainly owed much to the fact that King Robert I, "the Bruce", died of leprosy.

Scots law ordained that any leper who could not afford treatment in hospital was to receive money and was to be cared for at the public expense. Moreover, both municipal authorities and charitable organisations established asylums and hospitals for lepers all over Scotland. Notable in this respect was the Order of Saint Lazarus of Jerusalem whose greatest hospital in Scotland was probably that in Elgin, where "the leper lands" are still feued by the Burgh Council and where Lazarus Lane, leading to the cathedral, shows where seven of the Order's chaplains had their manses.

There is a common belief that the many Libertons in Scotland owe their name to their having formerly held 'Lepers' Towns' or colonies. This derivation is incorrect—unfortunately, for it is a pleasant notion. The 'Liber-' part of the name, however, has nothing to do with lepers, but comes from the old word *leber,* which means 'rushes'.

Devoted priests administered the Sacraments to lepers in the hospitals. In the countryside, where lepers were obliged to refrain from mixing with the people, for fear of spreading the disease, it was not possible for them to enter the churches during the time of service. At the same time, though, Christian charity took care that the lepers should not be deprived of the comforts of religion which, in many cases, must have been the only comforts upon which they could rely. Accordingly, special windows were cut into the walls of the churches, allowing the lepers a place where they could stand, outside the church, able to watch the service and to observe the Elevation of the Host.

These 'squinches' or 'Squints', from which lepers could see the altar, are still apparent in many Scottish churches which were built before the Reformation. They are still there, although, for the comfort of the congregation, they have all been glazed or else built-in.

The Deid Bell, Brechin Cathedral

THE DEID BELL

Ling! Lang! Leid! Oor cat's deid!
Whit did she dee o'? A sair heid!
A'ye what ken't her when she wis alive,
Come tae the fun-eer-i-al at hauf-past five!

I have no idea where or when I learned that rhyme. It was many years ago, though, and I well remember how we children found that it satisfied all our needs for a war-chant, and how we used to drive our wretched parents almost demented as we paraded around the house, singing it and clanging an old hand-bell to mark the time. Apparently the rhyme still appeals to children, for it is not so long since I heard it sung by small girls, skipping to its rhythm, at the foot of Edinburgh's Canongate.

The words of the rhyme refer to a very ancient Scottish custom, when it was customary for the parish beadle to give notice of a forthcoming funeral, calling through the streets and ringing a special bell to attract attention to his announcement. Another of his duties on such occasions was to lead the funeral procession, ringing his bell all the while in order to give warning of its passing.

In some of the larger parishes, in the cities, a special bellman was appointed, and a curious superstition attached to his office. The bellman, according to belief, could expect an extra long and unusually active life. This was certainly the case with William Eadie, bellman of the Canongate, who died in November 1731 at the age of 120 years. It was said of him that he had buried the inhabitants of the Canongate thrice, that he was ninety years a freeman of the burgh and that he had married a second wife, "a lusty young woman", after he was a hundred years old.

Some few of the old Deid Bells have survived the years. That in Brechin Cathedral is of a design which appears to indicate that it was cast in the early 1500s, though the first mention of it, in the minutes of the Kirk Session, is in 1624. In 1648 the kirk officer, one John Mill, was authorised to engage "a helper, both in making of the graves, ringing of the great bell, and carrying the hand-bell through the town before the dead."

The crier's tongue has been silent for many years, and the note of his bell has not been heard for a long, long time. It is strange that the voices of children at play should still give a faint echo of their summonses.

SANCTUARY GARTH
THE STOB CROSS, *(Merkinch, Fife. A.911)*

SANCTUARY

Autre temps, autre moeurs—in the days when men lived roughly, their justice tended to match the times and was both rough and summarily inflicted. In those times, the Church alone preached of the quality of mercy and matched its teaching by surrounding its precincts with sanctuaries in which fugitives could find shelter until they were brought properly to trial. These sanctuaries of the Church existed all over Scotland and, indeed, all though Christendom.

Probably because the King received ecclesiastical annointment, sanctuary extended to the royal presence. It is still legally extant within the bounds of Holyroodhouse, although it is limited to debtors and has become ineffective since the abolition of imprisonment for debt.

One of the oldest of Scotland's sanctuaries, still marked out, is that which attached to the ancient church of Markinch, in Fife, which was traditionally founded by St Drostan, a prince of the Blood Royal and a nephew of St Columba. The Church was given to the Culdee community of Loch Leven, nearly a thousand years ago, and afterwards passed to the Roman Church.

In order that refugees should be able to recognise the places of sanctuary, the "garths" or borders of the areas were marked out with prominent signs. These did not only allow the man, who was pursued, to know that he had reached safety, but also served notice upon his pursuers that they faced severe penalties if they dared to continue their chase.

At Holyroodhouse, the boundary of the sanctuary garth is shown clearly in the cobblestones, where the Canongate joins the immediate approach to the Palace grounds. Another mark-stone, known as the Stob Cross, stands on the hill that overlooks Markinch. This is the survivor of a number of similar stones which, formerly, girded the whole region.

Neither rank nor wealth was protection from the penalties that attached to a breach of the Church's law of sanctuary. Even the King himself was not excepted. Thus it was that King Robert I was subjected to the extreme penalty of excommunication and an interdict was placed upon the whole of his realm, as a result of his slaying the Red Comyn at Dumfries, in 1306. The Bruce was not adjudged guilty of murder. The grievous nature of his crime did not lie in the killing (which he might have pleaded to be a judicial act of execution) but in the fact that it took place within a church and thus within the bounds of sanctuary.

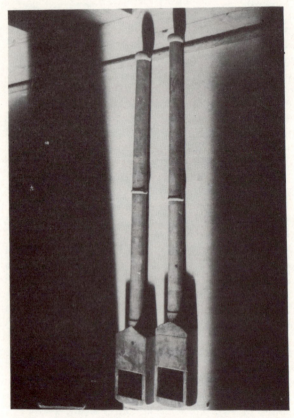

KIRK LADLES *(Logierait, Perthshire. A.827)*

KIRK LADLES

Recent difficulties caused by the change from £.s.d. to decimal currency are nothing compared with those which arose as a direct result of the Anglo-Scottish Treaty of Union, in 1707, when the new sterling currency was introduced throughout the newly-formed United Kingdom. Both new and old coins were in circulation at the same time, whilst things were made even more complicated by reason of the far-wandering habits of the Scottish people, who brought foreign money home with them.

Nowhere were the problems of coinage more acute than they were in the churches. Members of the congregation were inclined to place any coin that came to hand into the collection-bag—and some of those coins were of incredibly small value. Indeed, things came to such a pitch that, during the latter years of the 18th century and the first part of the 19th century, some parishes found it necessary to put their 'dud' coins into a different bag when, instead of passing it to the bank, they sold it by weight as scrap-metal!

In order that they might keep some check on what was being donated, some churches had wooden ladles made. These were carried round by the elders who were taking up the collection. The ladles had long handles, by which the elder would pass them along the pews, hoping that they might see bad coins when they were being deposited or else that they might be able to detect them by their sound as they landed on the wood.

Some parishes have retained their ladles in use today. Buckieburn Church, in St Ninian's Parish at Stirling, is one such, Minto Church near Hawick and Trinity Gask at Auchterarder are others. Many churches, who have adopted plates or bags for the collections, have yet kept their old ladles and display them as a reminder of past days and former customs. Ladles hang on the wall of Insh Kirk in Badenoch (though their handles have been shortened) and also at Logierait in Perthshire, where the pair illustrated were photographed.

MORTSAFES. *Logierait, Perthshire*
(O.S. Sheet 49: 968520)

THE BODY SNATCHERS

At the beginning of the last century, the medical schools of anatomy were in great difficulty to obtain sufficient subjects for dissection, for the only corpses that the law permitted them to use were those of paupers and those of criminals who had been hanged. Even in England the problem was acute, although that country possessed no more than two Universities and the English courts dealt out sentences of death in great numbers.

Scotland's medical schools were in far more trouble than those of England. Not only were there twice as many Universities, but the Scots law held only a fraction of the number of capital offences that existed under the English code. Scottish judges, moreover, were largely averse to pronouncing the death sentence, save for the gravest of crimes and in recidivist cases. The punishments most frequently inflicted in Scotland were those of banishment furth of the offender's burgh or county and, in serious offences, beyond the Scottish borders. Because of these circumstances, a flourishing trade arose in bodies, stolen from graveyards.

The most notorious of the "resurrectionists" who traded in human bodies for dissection were, of course, Burke and Hare. These two Irish scoundrels, however, were not content to wait for people to die in order to provide themselves with bodies—they committed murders.

Several methods were devised to foil the body-snatchers in Scotland. Watch-houses, with loopholed walls, were built to overlook the graveyards in order that armed sentries might keep guard over the newly-filled graves. Many of these watch-houses may be seen all over Scotland, one of the most notable being that which stands beside St Cuthbert's Church, in the centre of Edinburgh.

Another method of protecting the bodies, which met with considerable success, was the provision of iron cages which were buried together with the coffins.

These cages were immensely heavy, made of iron bars, usually by the local smith although it is known that they were also produced in quantity by several firms of iron-founders.

Known as Mortsafes, they covered the coffin and, in the narrow space provided by a grave, it was impossible for them to be lifted unless a powerful tackle was used—and that, of course, was impracticable for men working stealthily and at night.

Graves with mortsafes were, at first, filled in lightly. Then, when time had rendered the corpses useless for the purposes of the body-snatchers, the graves were again opened, the mortsafes removed and then, finally, the graves were permanently closed.

The mortsafes, which were expensive to manufacture, were usually the property of the parish and were kept in the graveyards, in a specially-built enclosure, ready for use whenever they should be needed. They are not uncommon, even today, though there are fewer than might be expected.

THE MURDERER'S HIDEOUT, *Tomintoul—Cock Bridge (A.939)*
(O.S. Sheet 38: 223153)

A VISITOR FROM THE SOUTH

Late in the Spring of 1920, a wanderer made his way northwards along the old military road towards Tomintoul in Banffshire. He passed the Soldiers' Well, some distance south of the township, and found an empty cottage. Quite casually and without asking permission of anyone, he took up his residence there. Nobody seems to have bothered much about him. He was just accepted amongst the hospitable Highland folk and although his strong English accent made it difficult for people properly to understand all that he said, he found little difficulty in obtaining casual employment with local farmers.

So things rested for several weeks, and then the police received a report that the stranger was tearing down the woodwork in the cottage where he had "squatted" and that he was burning it. The constable went out from Tomintoul to investigate and he took two of his neighbours with him for company. They had a startling reception. As they approached the cottage, they were met with a volley of revolver shots and both of the policeman's companions were wounded.

The man fled. The constable, however, was able to give a very accurate description of him and he was immediately recognised as an escaped criminal, named Topliss, who was badly wanted for the murder of a taxi-driver at Andover, in Hampshire. He had made good his escape from the English police and, by some means or another, had found his way into the Highlands. There he might still have been living, if he had not panicked when he saw the policeman and his friends approaching.

Nothing more was heard of him until nearly a week later. By that time he had made his way into the south where, between Penrith and Carlisle, a constable spotted him, recognised and challenged him. He drew his revolver and fired one round, but he missed and the policeman succeeded in getting away untouched, to call for armed assistance. This came quickly, and the peaceful countryside of Cumberland was enlivened by the unusual spectacle of a pistol duel on the highway. Topliss was shot dead by one of the police officers.

For some months, the cottage beside the Tomintoul to Cock Bridge road was something of a spectacle for gaping visitors. They soon wearied of it, though, and although the cottage still stands by the wayside, just as Topliss left it, the story which once filled the newspaper headlines has now been forgotten by almost everyone, and the tourists' cars drive past without stopping. Only a few of the local residents still remember the murderer whose guilty conscience led him to give himself away.

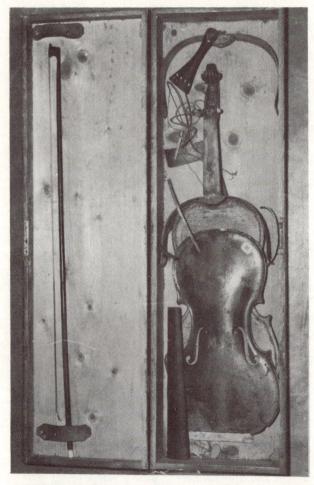

JAMES MACPHERSON'S FIDDLE. *Clan Macpherson Museum, Newtonmore, Inverness-shire. A.9.*

THE FREEBOOTER'S FIDDLE

"There's some cam' here tae see me hanged
An' some tae buy my fiddle,
But lang e'er I shall part wi' her,
I'll brak her i' the middle."

He tak the fiddle intae his haun,
He's brak it ower a stane,
"Nae ither haun shall gar her sing
When I am deid and gane,"

Sae rantinly, sae wantonly,
Sae dauntonly gaed he—
He played a tune and he daunced it roun'
Aneath the gallows-tree.

Macpherson's Rant is a well-known ballad with many versions, but few who sing or listen to it know that it tells of something which actually happened.

James Macpherson was the son of Macpherson of Invereshie and a beautiful girl of a tinker family. As a young man he made himself head of a wandering party of freebooters who were notable for their "Robin Hood" customs of taking from the rich and giving to the poor. They were, indeed extremely popular, which explains the manner in which James was enabled to escape from custody on several occasions when he had been arrested by authority.

Eventually he was brought to trial at Banff and, charged with a long series of armed robberies, he was condemned to be hanged after a trial which has a place in Scottish legal history on account of it having been the last ever to have been held under the old laws of Heritable Jurisdiction.

Hangings were not over frequent in Scotland, even in those days when severe punishments were more often imposed than they are today. Banishment was a more normal penalty for many offences which, in England, would have called for the death sentence. So it was that an appeal was lodged and there was every reason to believe that James's sentence had been commuted to one of banishment and that a messenger was actually on his way with the news.

Banff's authorities were determined that James should not escape. They had caught him (through the treachery of someone whom he had every reason to trust), they had managed to hold him, where others had been unable to keep him and they were going to take every possible step to ensure that he was not released. They effectively achieved their purpose by setting the town clock forward and hanging him when the hour struck, before any messenger could arrive.

During his last minutes of life, James played his fiddle at the foot of the gallows and then, when the time came for him to climb the ladder, he offered the instrument to anyone in the crowd who would accept it. Nobody dared to take it and he broke it over his knee and threw the pieces away amongst the people who were crowded around.

The bits of the broken fiddle were gathered up and later passed into the hands of the chief of Clan Macpherson, Cluny. Some years ago, when the effects of Cluny Castle were being sold by auction, the fiddle was bought by the Clan Macpherson Association, who preserve it in the Clan Museum at Newtonmore.

The ballad, telling of James Macpherson's death, is of unknown composition. Many people have adapted the words to their own tastes—Robert Burns amongst them. The tune to which it is sung is reputed to have been composed by James Macpherson himself and to have been the actual air that he played "Aneath the gallows tree". It has been set for playing on the pipes and, when I served in the Queen's Own Cameron Highlanders in the days before the last war, I was told that there was a Regimental tradition that *Macpherson's Rant,* sometimes called *Macpherson's Lament,* should never be played by our pipe band. Nobody could tell me the reason for the banning of the tune—it was 'just one of those things'.

MACPHERSON'S "FINGAL"
Title-page of the First Edition (1762)

OSSIAN

Modern research has largely confounded the critics, notably led by Dr Johnston, who maintained that Ossian never lived. It is generally agreed that the poet lived in the third century and that his heroes were real people—although many of their deeds were "written up" to make a good story.

Even today, Ossian's poems are recited in the Highlands and Islands by people who have learned them orally, in the traditional way. But their epics are not limited to Gaelic lore as is shown by references which go back to the days of Alexander II. Written in the Scots tongue, mention of Ossianic heroes and of the places where they lived shows that the tales form a part of the traditional lore of all Scotland, even though the actual poems have been preserved only in the Gaelic-speaking parts of the country.

It was not until 1762 that the world outside Scotland came to learn of Ossian. In that year, James Macpherson produced the first volume of his paraphrases of Ossian's poems, which he entitled "Fingal". Macpherson, somewhat naughtily, claimed that his books were translations. They were not that, but were productions which gave the general meaning of the Ossianic verses, told in Macpherson's own words and with additions of his own, which he inserted in order to support his belief that the poems had originally formed part of a single epic, comparable to the Odyssey.

Be that as it may, Macpherson's rendering of Ossian's poems brought about a literary revolution. From his books sprang the Romantic Movement which, within a few years, transformed all European literature and inspired some of the greatest musicians. The results are still with us. Seldom can the work of any one man have achieved so great a cultural result in so short a time as did that of James Macpherson. Still less frequently can a poet have so sprung to universal fame as did Ossian, eighteen centuries after his death.

As a postscript, it may be noted that Napoleon carried a volume of Ossian everywhere on his campaigns, and it was these poems that persuaded him to re-establish the Scots College in Paris, which had been destroyed at the Revolution.

CLACH NA BRATAICH. *Clan Donnachaidh (Robertson)*
Talisman since 1314. Clan Donnachaidh Museum, near the
Falls of Bruaŕ, beside the A.9, a few miles north of Blair
Atholl.
(O.S. Sheet 48: 821659)

CLAN DONNACHAIDH—THE ROBERTSONS

Clan Donnachaidh, whose Chief takes his territorial title from Struan, in Atholl, has many claims to fame. It is unique, too, amongst Highland Clans for, whilst taking pride in its ancient Gaelic name, it prides itself, too, on its Scots name of Robertson. It has very good reason for that pride because, according to the unchallenged tradition of the Clan, it was bestowed upon them by the King as a lasting memorial to Clan Donnachaidh's gallantry at Bannockburn. He accorded them the right to rank themselves as his own family, calling themselves by his own name, Robert's sons.

In 1969, after tremendous efforts, the Clan built itself a fine museum in which is displayed a splendid, constantly growing collection of relics which tell of the Clan's history.

In the museum are, naturally, many reminders of the Jacobite Risings. These include a coatee of Clan Robertson's tartan which was worn by Prince Charles himself at a ball in 1745, together with a pair of his shoe-buckles. Bagpipes played at the Battle of Prestonpans by a Robertson piper are there as is also another reminder of the same battle, acquired in a curious manner. This is a fiddle, believed to have belonged to General Sir John Cope, ('Johnnie Cope' of the Highland Regiments' reveillé), in whose captured coach the veteran Struan Robertson travelled home after the victory.

Most precious of all Clan Donnachaidh's possessions, though, is their magic stone, *Clach na Brataich* or Stone of the Banner. This is the Clan's talisman, to possession of which all their fortunes are tied, today as they have been for more than six centuries—for it is known to have been in the possession of the Struan family from at least 1314 and it is probable that they owned it even earlier than that year.

THE EILDON HILLS, *Roxburghshire, near Melrose. (A.68, A.6091, A.699, and many other roads)*

HILLS OF FAERY

It needs a very insensitive soul to look at the triple hills of Eildon and to remain unmoved. At all seasons and in all lights, the hills breathe peace and beauty over a landscape that has known its full share of war and trouble, no less than of gentleness and peace. Sir Walter Scott loved them and told of how, climbing to their tops, he could point out forty-three places, all famous in war and in verse. Close to their shadow lie, too, the great Abbeys and the rich farming lands which the old monks reclaimed from forest and marsh. The Eildons breath romance, and their romance is one with with great tale of the Borderlands.

It was by the Eildon tree that True Thomas met his lady, who took him into her own mystic country, whence he returned home with the powers of prophecy which, in his own rhyming couplets, are still quoted. Arthur himself, with his heroes around him, lies secure beneath Eildon, waiting for the call which will surely bring him back to rescue his country in her last and most grievous peril.

Old legend tells that the Eildons were one single hill until Michael Scott, the great wizard of the Borders, enlisted the Devil's help to split them into three. Legend, though, is not always true and, in this case, it is certainly false. Long before the days of Michael Scott, the Romans came to Eildon and called it *Trimontium* when they built their great encampment on the north-eastern peak.

The Eildons were sacred hills long before the Romans came to Caledonia. The old gods were worshipped in their high places and something of the mystery of those days still clings to the triple heights, enhancing the glamour and underlying the romance.

AM FEADAN DUBH, *The Black Chanter of Clan Chattan.*
In the Clan Macpherson Museum, Newtonmore (A.9)

THE BLACK CHANTER

The Highland bagpipes have played on very many battlefields but
seldom more strangely than at the Battle of the North Inch when, in
1396, Clan Chattan and Clan Kay were ordered to settle their differences
by armed combat in Perth, in the presence of King Robert III. Sir Walter
Scott has told the tale, elaborated with all the force of his romantic
imagination, in *The Fair Maid of Perth,* and his account is probably the
best known.

Clan Chattan, of course, still exists. It is a league of associated Clans
in the Central Highlands, with Macpherson and Mackintosh leading.

The identity of Clan Kay has been much disputed. I, personally, lean
to the view that it was the Clan Davidson which formed part of what
was termed 'The Old Clan Chattan', which made strong and bellicose
claim to seniority in the Chattan federation and whose Gaelic name is
Dhai, which is pronounced with a gutteral initial 'ghai'. That pronuncia-
tion is difficult enough for many Scots whilst for an Englishman it is
impossible. The name could very easily be mis-spelled as 'Kay' in a pho-
netic transliteration made by a southerner.

Several relics of the battle are kept in Clan Chattan and include the massive claymore, held by Mackintosh of Mackintosh at Moy Hall (*see page*). More notable, though, is the bagpipe chanter, of which many tales are told, which belongs to the Clan Macpherson.

The legend of *Am Feaden Dubh,* (the Black Chanter) begins in the Battle of the North Inch, when Clan Chattan's men were being forced back. Suddenly, music was heard in the clouds overhead and a chanter dropped from the sky. It fell at the feet of the Macpherson piper, who screwed it into his own pipes and, with its music, played the Clan to victory.

This tale, it must be admitted, is only one of several—most of which seem to contradict each other. This, however, is the version which is maintained by Clan Macpherson. Every Macpherson believes that the fortunes of his Clan are assured by the possession of *Am Feadan Dubh* and, with it, that other palladium of the Clan, *Am Bratach Uaine,* the Green Banner. Indeed, the Macpherson claims for the power of the Black Chanter go even further, for the Clan believes firmly that whoever holds the Chanter, even if it should be only on loan, will never be beaten in battle.

In evidence of the Chanter's powers, Macphersons quote the fact that it was lent to the Grants a short while before the Fifteen and remained with them until 1821. This, the Clan maintains, is the reason for the failure of both the Risings of 1715 and the Forty-five and the consequent disasters. After its return to the Chief, Clan Macpherson returned to its former eminence under Ewen Macpherson of Cluny, still remembered affectionately as 'Old Cluny'. Misfortune again struck the Clan when, once more, the Chanter passed out of its possession and a nadir was reached when, finally in 1943, Cluny Castle and all its treasures were sold by public auction.

After the sale, misfortune was again reversed, for the Black Chanter and, too, the Green Banner passed back into Macpherson hands when a loyal body of clansmen established the Clan Macpherson Association and successfully acquired these treasures of the Clan, together with several other relics of their history. The Head of the Clan, son of a man who had been "disinherited" and had emigrated, was succeeded after a short interregnum, by the late Brigadier Alan Macpherson of Cluny and Blairgowrie, much-beloved and one of the very few Highland Chiefs who maintained his home in Scotland.

The Clan is now one of the few which owns part of its ancient homeland as a corporate body. Its Museum, in Newtonmore, houses a wonderful and increasing collection of the Clan's historic treasures amongst which, of course, pride of place is given to the Black Chanter to whose recovery is attributed all this new and continuing success.

CAPSTAN FOR HORSE-DRIVEN WINNOWING FANS *at Ballachroan, near Newtonmore, Inverness-shire*

BALLACHROAN HOUSE *near Newtonmore, Inverness-shire. Footpath from A.9.*
(O.S. Sheet 37: 733003)

THE DEVIL AT BALLACHROAN

Th e house of Ballachroan stands between Newtonmore and Kingussie, hidden by a slope from the A.9 highway less than a quarter of a mile away. It is reputed to have been the first two-storey building in Badenoch and it has even been claimed that, when it was built in the late 1700s, it was the only double-storied house between Blair Atholl and Inverness. Nowadays, it stands unoccupied and roofless. There is a heavy and gloomy atmosphere about the whole place, which would certainly discourage anyone from making a home there. Among the people who know the house, there are few who do not believe it to be haunted and I am prepared to believe them—although the only frightening thing that I have met there, for myself, was a huge wildcat which had made its den under the rotting beams of the floor.

Ballachroan's eerie reputation is not surprising, considering that it was built by Captain John Macpherson, *an Oichear Dubh*—the Black Officer—who was firmly believed to be a close friend of the Devil. In some ways, the captain may be said to have brought his reputation upon his own head, for he had made himself hugely unpopular by his energetic, unscrupulous and even dishonest methods of raising recruits to fight in the French wars. Having given himself a bad name, no accusation was too imaginative to be raised against him and, too, to be believed.

During three years, the crops at Ballachroan surpassed any other that were grown in the district. People refused to believe that this could have been achieved by natural means. Only assistance from the Devil would have brought about such phenomenal results. This just shows the perversity of the human mind, which attributed good results to diabolic assistance whilst, even today, assures us that disasters are acts of God! However, so the story arose and, within a very few years, was being told with an accumulated wealth of detail.

The Devil gives nothing without obtaining something in exchange. In the first year of his bargaining with the Black Officer, he promised that Ballachroan should have splendid crops—provided that he, himself, should be given whatever grew above ground. The captain agreed—and, instead of planting bear or oats as did the other farmers, he planted neeps. All that the devil received was a stack of shaws.

In the next year, the Devil made the same bargain but, not to be out-done a second time, he demanded that he should receive all that grew underground for his share. This time, though, the Black Officer sowed grain—and all that Satan received was stubble and roots.

When the third year came around, the Devil made certain that his part of the bargain should show a profit. He demanded all that could be enclosed within diagonal lines drawn from corner to corner across the fields. Again the bold Macpherson agreed. This time, though, he planted nothing. Instead of growing crops, he fattened cattle. And, instead of keeping the cattle in the fields, he made circular enclosures of hurdles, which he moved from place to place as the grazing was used up. With no proper fields and with no corners to the temporary fields, no diagonals could be drawn . . . and the Devil received even less than he had in either of the preceding years!

The tale used to be believed completely and even today there are people who refuse altogether to discredit it. One part of the story is perfectly true, for it is a fact that the Black Officer's crops were far, far better than those obtained by anyone else in the district. His success, though, was not due to diabolic assistance, but was the result of his own skill and ingenuity. You see, John Macpherson of Ballachroan was the first man, living locally, ever to use a proper rotation of crops in his system of farming.

Just outside the barn at Ballachroan, one relic still remains to show how advanced the Black Officer was in his methods, compared with other farmers in Badenoch at the end of the 18th century. On a mound is a cross-shaped iron casting with sockets to take shafts of capstan-bars. Horses or oxen were harnessed to these and driven round and round, turning the shaft which, connected by a system of rods and gears, drove a winnowing-fan inside the barn, where the remains of the machinery can still be seen. Even this simple and practical machine stood against him in the district, however. The ministers and the elders of the Kirk maintained that the making of winds was a prerogative of the Lord, so that any notion of raising winds by artificial means was an impiety which amounted almost to blasphemy. With the bad reputation that the Black Officer had won, he just couldn't win, whatever he did.

Let us agree, in the light of our modern knowledge, that the wind that winnowed the chaff at Ballachroan was raised by a simple mechanical tool and not through a blasphemous assumption of the powers of God; and let us agree, too, that he obtained his excellent crops by his application of modern agricultural methods before they had become generally known in the Highlands. There are other stories about the Black Officer which are not so easily explained. Who, for instance, was his Visitor, who left no tracks in the snow when he come to the door of Ballachroan at the New Year of 1799? What were the circumstances of his death in the storm which brought in the year of 1800? What were the mysterious happenings which are said to have hindered the recovery of his body? There are many stories about *an Oichear Dubh*, which are still told and still believed. These, though, are for the ceilidh by the fire on winter nights . . .

INDEX